Jorge Mendoza Vester

The Secrets of the Great Esoteric Tarot

ecovisiones

Jorge Mendoza Vester is an economist and holds a master's degree in philosophy.

He directed the Ecovisiones Magazine, where he disseminated systemic and holistic thinking through articles such as Alchemy, Biochemistry, and Immortality; Reality or Realities; How to Live Better with Less.

He has practiced tarot for over thirty years and, as a teacher, has trained countless tarot readers in workshops and seminars.

Together with Daniel Rodes, Encarna Sanchez, and Christine Payne-Tawler, he belongs to a generation of new tarotists who follow in the footsteps of the tradition of Eliphas Levi, Oswald Wirth, and Maritxu Guler.

In his vision of tarot, he has sought to provide historical rigor, systematicity, and scientific foundation to its study, drawing on systems theory and neurolinguistic programming. In this way, he has succeeded in making tarot learning accessible to people with different levels of education and skills.

In 'The Secrets of the Great Esoteric Tarot,' he exposes the keys to this intriguing deck full of symbolic content. Drawing on tradition and the Basque-Navarrese culture of the author, he reveals the mysteries of its arcana, opening paths for those who want to initiate and delve deeper into this tarot.

Currently, the author works as a political science teacher at the University Mayor."

Índice

Introduction

The first tarot deck that came into my hands was the one known as the Great Esoteric Tarot (GET). This deck attracted me from the moment I held it. The simplicity of its well-defined lines, set against a clean white background, enclosed a sophisticated symbolism that I gradually came to understand. From the beginning, I found in it a mysterious aura that fascinated me.

The deck is enigmatic, differing in some respects from a traditional Marseille deck, and it also explicitly incorporates symbolism that is only attributed by scholars to traditional decks, but which the creators of such decks do not present in their images.

Back then, in the mid-eighties of the last century, there was not much information about tarot, and about the Great Esoteric Tarot, there was simply none. However, I was fortunate enough to get my hands on a copy of Eliphas Levi's "Dogma and Ritual of High Magic." The book included images, and one of the figures in this book seemed suspiciously familiar to the Arcanum number XV, Aker, of this deck. So, with this book and the instruction booklet that came with the cards, signed by Maritxu Guler, I dedicated myself to getting to know my new deck.

The truth is that, apart from the help provided by Levi's book, there was little I could decipher at first. I progressed in creating a specific spread for this deck, but its peculiarities and secrets continued to be a mystery to me. Only in the last two decades, with the help of the Internet, the work of some prominent tarot readers, and meticulous research, have I managed to shed light on specific aspects of the GET that add so much flavor.

In my journey through bookstores, libraries, and now on the web, I have not been able to find specific material about this deck, but what I have seen are many questions from interested parties wanting to know the specific details of the cards. Unfortunately, the answers almost all refer back to the instruction booklet that comes with the deck and do not provide further information. I say unfortunately, as the descriptions that appear there are generic, as befits a promotional brochure, and they do not delve into what is unique to the GET, much less contain a description of the overall plan of the deck.

With this perspective in mind, I believe that the presentation of information about the peculiarities of this deck covers an aspect that is not currently available. The information I present in these pages covers both the specific aspects of the cards, as well as the set of interrelationships contained in the GET that I have not seen in other decks.

The central aspects of the GET allow for a detailed examination and a systemic presentation of its structural characteristics that are so at hand in the deck, helping to clarify the relational aspects found in the foundations of any deck that follows the general lines of a Marseille Tarot.

Therefore, reading this work is not only useful for those specifically interested in the GET, but it can also be beneficial for anyone who wants to delve deeper into their knowledge of tarot and go beyond a basic or memorized understanding of the cards, approaching them from the relationships that can be established with them, so that in this way, the cards begin to speak to us.

I believe this material can be of particular interest to all those users and scholars of the Marseille Tarot and decks derived from it, because a large amount of information, which could only be hinted at in the time it was created, easily and explicitly springs forth from the study of the GET.

A recent group of tarotists and tarot writers have begun to rescue and give relevance to the main aspects of the tarot tradition. Among them are Carlo Bozelli, Daniel Rodés and Encarna Sánchez, Francisco Benages, Christine Payne Towler, to name those with published books, although it is also possible to find other authors who have taken up this challenge on numerous web pages.

The characteristic of the mentioned authors is that they conceive the tarot as a complex system of relationships through its arcana, which in turn possesses a profound simplicity, accessible to anyone who approaches it with an open mind and free of prejudice.

Rodés and Sánchez (2014) propose laws for the interpretation of the cards, such as the law of looks or the law of repetition, among others. Bozzelli (2014), also proposes laws and codes such as the law of antithesis, law of duality, law of duplicity, and models for its understanding like the historical and the esoteric. Benages (2016), incorporates innovative theoretical approaches such as coaching, Neuro-Linguistic Programming, and outlines the theory of systems.

In the case of Christine Payne-Towler (2016), she provides an erudite and accessible view of the historical origins and influence of different schools and currents of thought on the configuration of the decks considered traditional, which is complementary to that of the previous authors.

In all of them, the common pattern is the incorporation of meta-models that give the tarot an omni-comprehensive approach, a holistic view that is its basic essence. If we wanted to refer to a modern approach within scientific disciplines that support this vision, the obligatory reference is the General Systems Theory[1] coined by the Austrian Ludwig von Bertalanffy in the first half of the 20th century. This approach, after its formulation, has had multiple developments in various disciplines, proving its explanatory capacity time and again. Of special mention, for its interest in this study, is the presence of the GST in psychology and administration. In both sciences, it has proven its usefulness when applied to the understanding of human groups due to its emphasis on the relational aspects of human interaction.

In psychology, the most promising approaches of this science, which have moved away from psychoanalysis, have incorporated GST as the backbone of their theories. In the field of management, GST is an essential part of its basic teaching cycle, which, by incorporating it into the study of all types of organizations, has gained a theoretical approach to begin to establish itself as a

---

1. "From now on, I will use the acronym 'GST' to refer to 'General Systems Theory'.

scientific discipline.

The reasons mentioned lead to considering GST as a powerful tool for approaching tarot, given that, on one hand, it is consistent with its traditional aspects and on the other, it refreshes it by updating it with modern views on the understanding of human beings.

For this reason, I incorporate the systems approach as an indispensable tool in the teaching of tarot, and I dedicate a significant number of pages to this in this work. The reader interested in the specific aspects of the GET who wishes to skip the aspects of GST can do so, although I personally recommend reading its basic conceptual aspects, since even this approach will significantly enrich the practical use of the cards in reading.

The incorporation of GST for learning tarot provides it with a conceptual framework that was always implicit in the tradition and updates its teaching to modern language, additionally bringing the tarot closer to a scientific approach, distancing it from the charlatanism that sometimes accompanies it, without losing any of its essence.

These introductory topics seek to provide a conceptual framework and a systematic approach for a better understanding of the GET, however, the bulk of this book is dedicated to what its title indicates: the Great Esoteric Tarot.

The journey I undertake on this aspect begins with the origin of the GET, the sources to which its authors refer: this is the central factor in this section. Clarifying this point greatly facilitates the understanding of the detail of each of the arcana that make it up, as well as the projections that can be given to the deck, for example, regarding the spreads that can be derived from it.

A second point regarding the deck is the detailed examination of each of the arcana, meticulously studying their particularities. In this exploration, I always keep in mind the Marseille Tarot and compare each of the respective arcana with this canonical deck. This method sheds light on the similarities and differences that can be established in the cards.

Experience tells me that this method is very appropriate in the teaching of tarot. I have been using it in the workshops I teach, and for the students, it has been an educational resource that facilitates learning. Additionally, carrying out the comparative exercise provides the reader with a dual resource. On one hand, they access the contents of the GET and on the other, they obtain contents from the cards of the Marseille Tarot. This will allow them to reinforce what they already knew about this deck or to be introduced to it.

A final aspect that I explore in these pages is about the spreads. It is here where the skills of the tarot reader unfold, and finding a suitable spread, that matches the available abilities or the demands of the query, is an essential task. It is beneficial for a tarot reader to know more than one spread, as this will give them agility, confidence, and fluidity, and will allow them to easily adapt to the requirements of a consultation or a particular deck.

As part of the adventure undertaken in writing the book, I have developed a "spread" for this deck, based on its structure, along with its functional relationships. In my opinion, and based on my experience, I can say that it works very well, has been very satisfactory, and of great help. I also explore some traditional spreads, with examples, which will be a contribution for those who wish to familiarize themselves with this aspect of tarot.

Once the general plan of the work is presented, I invite readers to immerse themselves in the sheets of the Great Esoteric Tarot.

Origin of the Great Esoteric Tarot

The Great Esoteric Tarot was published in 1978, marking the 600th anniversary of the appearance of playing cards in Europe. The creation of the deck was commissioned by the playing card manufacturer Heraclio Fournier to a very special person in the Spanish esoteric world, Maritxu Guler, and Luis Peña Longa for the drawings. The deck is based on the Tarot of Marseille model but has a set of peculiarities that make it unique, for which its creators are responsible.

From an aesthetic point of view, the first thing that stands out in the GET is that the major and minor arcana are drawn on a white background with primary colors, where black, red, blue, and green predominate; this choice of colors makes it very striking and gives the cards a special appeal. The distribution of the 22 major arcana is almost the same as the Marseille one, except for The Fool, which is suggested to be placed as the penultimate card between The Cycle (Judgment in a Marseille Tarot) and The World.

I will leave the similarities there for now, as I will elaborate on them in detail later. The differences are varied, although they allow maintaining the general structure of a Marseille deck. Among the most significant modifications are the presence of the Hebrew alphabet[2] and astrological signs, the motifs of some of its cards, such as The Consultant for The Magician, or Aker, numbered XV and, therefore, corresponding to The Devil in the Tarot of Marseille, as the main ones.

This last arcana, Aker, gives us a significant clue about the tradition that its creators wanted to leave present in the deck, as it alludes to the land of origin of its creator.

---

2. "Although it might not be accurate to use the term 'alphabet', for simplicity's sake, I have chosen to use it."

About Luis Peña Longa, practically nothing is known about his personal life or his sources of inspiration. However, there is more information about Maritxu Guler, both in the instruction books that accompany the deck and about the context in which her life developed and the cultural context that inspired her work.

She was born in the village of Roncal in Navarra and was married to a Swiss man who supported her research in the world of esotericism and with whom she settled near San Sebastián in the Basque Country. She worked as a teacher and studied parapsychology in Paris.

In her lifetime, she was known as the good witch of Ulía, although she was not comfortable with this nickname. However, her personal characteristics of simplicity, discretion, and humility, as well as her perceptive and divinatory abilities, which even allowed her to intuit the death of some people in advance, make her a worthy heir to the sorginak[3] of the Basque Country, and no one better than Maritxu to carry that title.

These details, along with the reference she makes to Eliphas Levi in the instruction book of the deck, are key to understanding the concepts around which the deck is built.

Some of the cards have motifs inspired by the esoteric tradition of the Basque Country and Navarra, such as in the arcana XV Aker and The Tower. It's evident that Maritxu highlights these themes in her creation, drawing on the symbolism of her land and incorporating it into the GET, while respecting the general structure of a Marseille deck.

Another source she draws upon for the significant esoteric symbolism added corresponds to the studies of Eliphas Levi, which

---

3. "This expression comes from the Basque language and means 'witch' or 'woman of knowledge' in that language. According to magical-religious traditions, the sorginak would gather at night to celebrate the witches' sabbath led by a male goat. According to other versions, they are assistants of the goddess Mari, from the Basque tradition, in her fight to restore truth. In all cases, it is a matriarchal tradition of life, where the feminine has a special prominence."

Oswald Wirth[4] had already coined in a deck of his creation.

Finally, it's appropriate to add Maritxu Guler's own studies on symbolism, which are especially expressed in arcana I, The Magician, which in this deck is named The Consultant, and profusely in other cards of the deck. In the case of The Consultant, the inspiration clearly corresponds to "The man of Gichel", an image that illustrates a work on alchemy and Christian mysticism to which I will refer in more detail when analyzing this card.

Essentially, these are some of the inspiring sources that give origin to this very special deck, which I will examine in depth in the following pages. Of course, it is possible that I miss references that contributed to the elaboration of the deck; in fact, Maritxu left nothing in writing besides the brief instruction booklet that accompanies it, but I believe that these pages will contribute to unveiling part of the mysteries that accompany this deck, making it more accessible to the general public.

I consider this to be a valuable exercise, as in this tarot there is a great wealth of interpretative and symbolic richness explicitly, which is not usual in decks that follow the standard tradition.

---

4. Refer to (Wirth, 1990a) for further details.

Systemic Approach and Structure of Tarot

A common way to learn tarot is to understand the symbolism of each card and then apply it in practice. With this method, beginners often face many problems in their initial readings: inability to remember the meanings of the cards and other difficulties that create insecurity, and even when one becomes a seasoned tarot reader, they might still overlook one of the most important aspects of the cards' interpretative capacity, which is the overall vision of the situation.

In this case, the problem is not with the tarot reader, but with the learning method, because learning in this way has several limitations. Among these, the main one is that it neglects the synoptic view and the relational capacity that the cards offer. This is an essential aspect of tarot and corresponds to the worldview of its creators, who had in mind the work of the cathedral builders.

To facilitate the learning of tarot and achieve an understanding of its deeper aspects, I consider it appropriate to try to elucidate the original motivations of its creators. I know this is a virtually impossible task, as even if we had all the necessary materials for this examination, which we do not, we could not avoid looking with the eyes of the present at a tool that was created in another era with a different worldview, corresponding to the habits and customs of its creators. However, this does not prevent us from trying to approach some essential and underlying aspects in the structure and relational elements, which are probably universal and timeless.

Additionally, I will update the understanding of tarot with a contemporary perspective, incorporating new tools in its study that are also completely consistent with the relational structure of tarot. Within this analytical toolkit, the General Systems Theory is of special importance.

The origins of tarot are and will probably continue to be a matter of controversy, due to the scarcity of historical background because of the passage of time, the destruction of much material, Church censorship, and the fact that for a long period, its knowledge was linked to secret and initiatory societies, hence this information was kept secret due to the practices that characterize these organizations. However, the available evidence today indicates that tarot appeared in Europe in the early 15th century (Payne-Towler, n.d.), coinciding with the historical period known as the Renaissance (González, n.d., p. 5).

I consider this coincidence very appropriate, as the Renaissance shook the structures of feudalism, rescuing the wisdom, knowledge, and arts of classical antiquity. In parallel, there was a flourishing of and interest in ancient wisdom and mysticism, which is expressed in the aforementioned secret and initiatory societies.

If we consider the time when the first tarot decks appeared, according to what we know today, we can see that these coincide with the appearance of printing in Europe. The techniques that preceded printing coincide in time with the appearance of the oldest decks, and although these were hand-painted, later techniques that allowed for mass reproduction, such as woodcut[5], were incorporated in their reproduction.

The incorporation of these techniques caused the images of the cards to lose expressive richness, as engraving only allows the use of basic and flat colors. Today, this has been a controversial issue and some researchers have sought to restore to the tarot the richness of its original colors[6].

One of the most important aspects of the coincidence of the appearance of the tarot and the printing press is that at that time, written culture was a rare phenomenon and those who could read and write were few. Popular culture was transmitted as it

5. "Woodcut involves typographic printing using engraved wooden plates. This same technique allows for the reproduction of sheets like tarot cards."

6. "Woodcut involves typographic printing using engraved wooden plates. This same technique allows for the reproduction of sheets like tarot cards."

had traditionally been, through orality, and tales, stories, myths, and histories were the way culture was transmitted from one generation to another.

The tarot emerged before printed culture. In this world, the art of memory was still very important, and images played a very important role as a mnemonic resource. This aspect is clearly observed in the Visconti tarots, as the sheets have no name or number to identify them.

On the other hand, it is necessary to point out that decks prior to the tarot included in their set of sheets themes such as the gods of Olympus, professions, and other motifs around the social hierarchy of the time that seemed to fulfill an educational function. It is likely that these decks had a pedagogical support function. It is reasonable to consider that these first decks played this function, even a couple of centuries before the appearance of the first tarots in the 15th century.

The geographical setting in which this crystallizes is a specific area of Europe that includes northern Italy, France, and eastern Spain, which at that time was experiencing cultural turbulence, full of changes and richness of content.

Many of the motifs and symbols of the cards can be seen even today in the cathedrals of these places and throughout Europe. The universality and syncretism that the images of the cards contain correspond to the prevailing worldview at that time.

The moment when the cards appear in Europe is a point of encounter of worldviews that oppose each other in some aspects and complement each other in others. The predominant vision in the Middle Ages is mainly theocentric, and one of the turns that the Renaissance, with the influence of humanism, makes is to put the human being at the center.

But this aspect of the Renaissance is not the only one that interests us, as turning back to classical antiquity brings ancient texts of mysticism like the Corpus Hermeticum to light. Hermeticism and Neoplatonism are precursors to the secularization that begins to occur strongly among the main thinkers of the era. Among other aspects, this view conceives of the human being in harmony with nature, contemplates the aspects of life in close interrelation, and sees the human being as having great potential for development, capable of cultivating themselves in all aspects. Paraphrasing the architect Leon Battista Alberti, a prominent humanist of the cinquecento, among other things an architect, mathematician, philosopher, musician, and poet: the artist should not only be a mere craftsman, but an intellectual prepared in all disciplines and in all fields.

This way of conceiving the artist at that time, captures the main characteristics of Renaissance humanism, of which, probably its most iconic figure is Leonardo da Vinci. The universalist training of who has been considered one of the greatest artists of all time is admirable, but not exclusive. A significant number of artists, poets, philosophers, scientists of his time share this quality: a multifaceted and multidisciplinary education.

A broad education is consistent with the worldview that crystallizes in this era and that is the sum of medieval philosophy, the resurgence of classicism, and the new perspective that the Renaissance brings. This vision is captured by the creators of the tarot and consistently with it, they create, through successive approximations, a device in the form of a deck of cards in which there is a totality whose parts are interconnected. This perspective, as we will see, is fully consistent with Systems Theory.

Precisely, the richness of the tarot lies in its infinite creative capacity. From a few elements and a simple set of rules, it is capable of creating an entire universe. In this sense, it is equivalent to language and could also be explained with the tools of Noam Chomsky's generative grammar.

An old story I heard when I was taking my first steps with the cards, surely taken from another source and slightly modified as often happens with oral tradition, tells of a prisoner sentenced to life imprisonment who was granted the grace to request books. When asked for the list of books he would request, there was only one on it: a tarot deck. To the astonishment of the jailers, the prisoner pointed out that the tarot was enough for him, as it contained all the knowledge of the universe.

Beyond this anecdote[7], the extraordinary creative richness that the tarot provides for storytelling from a simple set of elements and rules lies in the multiplying power of the relationships that can be established among the components. While the elements are few, 22 if only the major arcana are considered or 78 if the entire deck is taken into account, the combinations that can be established between two or more cards, though not infinite, significantly increase the number of elements now considered as pairs (or groups of more than two) of cards, compared to if we restrict ourselves to the number of elements that make up the deck: the 78 cards[8].

The discipline (or approach) that systematically studies the relational properties of a set is Systems Theory, so in the following lines, I will present its general characteristics, keeping in mind its practical application in tarot.

---

7. "The story is narrated by Eliphas Levi in his book 'Dogma and Ritual of High Magic'.

8. According to combinatorial analysis, if we take groups of two cards, the possible combinations are: $78! \, / \, (2! * (78 - 2)!\,) = 3{,}003$.

Systemic Approach

Systems Theory is a new discipline that developed in the mid-20th century from the propositions of Ludwig von Bertalanffy. This scientist, drawing from his experience in biology, developed a new theoretical body, with a universal perspective and application in multiple disciplines.

Von Bertalanffy observed that the prevailing principles and methodological practices imposed limitations on scientific endeavors, particularly the reductionist and analytical view dominant in traditional science. To overcome this limited approach, he proposed the concept of a system, which comes from the Greek word σύστημα, meaning to gather, to place together. In other words, a system means an integrated whole whose fundamental properties lie in the relationships of its components. A good synthesis of the essence of systemic thinking is: the whole is more than the sum of its parts.

Systems theory and cybernetics share important aspects in their approaches and also many concepts, among which the following can be mentioned:

• Circularity: this concept is central in cybernetics and GST, and refers to processes that mutually feed each other. This concept changes the traditional view of causal relationships where B is a consequence of A (A -> B), but simultaneously A is also a consequence of B (A <-> B), therefore, the relationship can be represented in both directions and not just in a unidirectional sense.

This property of living systems is key for the existence of processes that repeat and reinforce themselves each time they occur, such as: John distrusts Peter, but this attitude of John makes Peter in turn observe that something strange is happening with John and therefore, he distrusts him, which causes him to act reservedly with John. By acting this way, Peter validates John's initial perception and thus allows the cycle to repeat and amplify each time they interact.

Situations similar to this hypothetical case are often seen in card readings. For example, someone consulting, caught in such a relationship, gets the major arcana The Tower. Generally, I interpret this card as the dissolution of a "project", which has positive connotations, because the project is an egocentric projection of the individual. If we take the Tower of Babel as a metaphor and remember that this building was intended to be built by the flood survivors to reach the sky, in punishment for their pride, the Bible says they were punished by multiplying the languages they spoke so they could no longer understand each other. Therefore, when such "projects" fail or end, it is positive for the consultant, because they are being freed from attitudes or a relationship that was limiting their personal growth or well-being.

The above is valid when the card is in an upright position, but when the card is reversed, it nullifies the positive interpretation and indicates that the consultant is clinging to that project and is trapped in a situation that possibly clouds their judgment and limits their possibilities of fully enjoying life.

• Emergence: this principle of GST refers to the fact that qualities and attributes are not based on the separate parts of a whole, for example, the cells that make up the liver, individually do not possess the properties that the organ has as a whole. If we place each of the cells that form the liver side by side, they do not constitute the organ. The liver appears in the relationships that the cells form with each other to constitute the organ in its entirety. This is one of the central concepts of GST. Among other things, because it explains the idea that the whole is more than the sum of its parts.

• Structure: Every system is made up of parts that compose it and also by the relationships that the components establish with each other to form a system. Some authors consider that only the components form the structure and prefer to consider the relationships between them as the organization.

Whatever definition is adopted, if we consider a flock of

sheep as a system, the sheep, calves, and the ram are the elements that make up that system, and for example, a sheep nursing its young is one of the relationships that constitute the system.

• Homeostasis: this concept is one of the most relevant of GST, especially for living organisms, although it also applies to social systems and various types of systems. Homeostasis occurs in response to modifications in the environment that affect a living being, which, in the face of changes in the environment, adjusts its internal structure, that is, makes internal changes in its system with the purpose of maintaining its organization unchanged. Autopoiesis, from the perspective of Humberto Maturana (2003), can be understood as the conservation of homeostasis.

• Organization: organization consists of the interrelations of the different elements that make up a system. The organization, by establishing the possibilities of a system, defines the possible states for that system, in other words, its universe of possibilities. This is a key concept to understand living beings, as these operate conserving or maintaining their organization, that is, the organization, in addition to establishing the possibilities of a living being, defines its identity and its belonging to a class or species.

• Negentropy: This is a concept that systems theory borrows from physics, particularly thermodynamics, which establishes some universal laws that are applicable in all types of processes. The first of these laws and the most well-known is the law of conservation of energy. The law that interests us for our purposes is the second law of this discipline. According to some interpretations, the second law of thermodynamics states that systems tend to states of more probable organization (entropy), and the most probable state of systems is disorder. Negentropy, on the contrary, refers to a special quality of open systems, the ability to incorporate additional energy into their structure to maintain their states of organization. This is what allows any living being to develop all its processes and maintain its main characteristic: life.

• Feedback: This property is closely related to homeostasis. Feedback consists of those processes through which an open system collects information from the environment, which allows it to adapt its internal processes to be compatible with the environment. Therefore, feedback affects the future actions of a living being; through it, systems modify their actions according to the collected information and do not remain fixed and static over time, invariant in a changing environment, as this would risk their existence.

In the realm of human interactions, we are in a process of permanent feedback; in fact, language is a recursive way of interacting in which we are systematically feeding back.

GST recognizes two types of feedback: negative feedback and positive feedback; their differences are significant enough to consider them separately.

○ Positive feedback refers to a sequence of circular relationships in which the change of one of its components is transmitted to other components of the system, amplifying the initial change. Positive feedback is present in phenomena of growth and differentiation. For example, it occurs in the growth of a living being, whether it is the leaf of a tree or a baby. From a tiny number of cells, these reproduce, multiply, and then differentiate from each other, creating organs that perform different functions, in a continuous process in which the living being grows in size until it reaches adulthood.

In the medium and long term, positive feedback processes tend to be stabilized by other processes that stop growth, because otherwise living beings would grow indefinitely.

A similar situation occurs with the number of individuals of a species in an ecological niche, which initially grows without restrictions, but there comes a time when this growth tends to be regulated by the scarcity of resources, the presence of predators, or other reasons. As a result, the number of individuals of the species in question remains stable within its environment, continuously making adjustments that enable the quantity to match the existing possibilities.

In the realm of human relationships, we find examples in jealous relationships, where one partner distrusts the other, the person who is the object of distrust feels suffocated in the relationship and seeks spaces of freedom, which in turn reinforces the distrust of the jealous person, and so the relationship continues to reinforce itself more and more in the distrust that jealousy implies.

It should be noted that not all positive feedback has negative consequences. On the contrary, there are many relationships that are positively reinforced and have positive results for those who experience them. For example, in a loving relationship, a gesture of affection and/or selflessness will predispose the recipient favorably and in turn, they will be willing to reciprocate with affectionate actions, creating a cycle of affectionate interactions that reinforce each other.

• Negative feedback corresponds to self-regulation processes in which the difference between an observed value and a predetermined value or range of values is reduced; such as body temperature, hence the concept of negative feedback is equivalent to homeostasis.

A classic example of negative feedback is automatic pilot or navigation systems, in which a course or destination is set, and the current course is periodically compared with the preset course. If there are differences between the two values, actions are taken to correct the course by reducing the existing difference between the preset course and the course obtained through measurement.

In personal relationships, distrustful relationships are "neutralized" with gestures of trust that can restore the balance of a couple's relationship.

As we can see, processes of positive and negative feedback are continually interacting and part of broader processes or with a longer time horizon.

GST has extensive conceptual development and, as noted, has contributed to the development of multiple scientific disciplines and is undoubtedly a promising theoretical body due to its conceptual richness, flexibility, and the multiple tools and possibilities it offers to researchers in any field.

Even though it may initially seem somewhat inaccessible, grounding it through examples, like the ones we have previously given about human relationships in general, allows us to assimilate and verify that we are using its concepts and analytical tools in our daily lives. Familiarizing ourselves with them enriches our possibilities in daily life and especially in the practice of tarot. In the following pages, I will provide examples applied to our topic of interest.

The depth and breadth of the conceptual body of GST prevents us from developing it in detail, but what we have seen so far is sufficient to provide us with a set of tools that will endow our understanding of the tarot with a new perspective that enriches how it is viewed. Central to this vision is the conception of phenomena in an interconnected, connected, interacting manner, forming part of a whole.

A Tarot card hardly explains itself alone; it requires an understanding of the cards that accompany it. Just as a card does not explain itself alone, the answers sought by the consultant are not found only within themselves but also in the network of relationships that accompany them in their daily life. The vision and tools provided by Systems Theory contribute to the tarot reader's immersion in the essence of the tarot according to a modern and systematic perspective.

Finally, I want to invite the reader to delve deeper into this subject, either through specialized works on the topic or through an upcoming publication that we are preparing.

Tarot Structure

As we have seen, the greatest potential of the tarot arises from the interrelation between the cards, and this emerges from the underlying structure within them. Therefore, we will now explore this structure, showing its most visible components as well as those more secretive aspects that only manifest after in-depth study.

The set of cards that has become standard or canonical as a tarot deck is a pack composed of 78 cards in total, 56 of them known as minor arcana and 22 as major arcana. There are other distributions of the cards, but generally, in decks considered as tarot, and following the pattern of the Tarot of Marseille, there are no significant deviations from the original structure.

The 56 minor arcana are divided into four suits, which in the Tarot of Marseille are coins, wands, cups, and swords. Each suit is composed of 16 cards, which can be divided into two groups, the first consisting of ten numbered cards from 1 to 10, and the other group made up of four court arcana: a page or valet, a knight, a queen, and a king.

In turn, the 22 major arcana have one unnumbered card (The Fool) and twenty-one numbered figures from 1 to 21. The symbolism of The Fool, its flexibility, ubiquity, and the fact that it is not numbered, has led most who theorize on the subject to consider that this arcana can take the place of any of the other twenty-one, or to travel a path through all of them. This is why The Fool, in the English deck known as the Joker, can replace any card in many of the games played with these cards, and for this reason, it is known as the wild card.

To better understand the major arcana, it is convenient, for the reasons previously explained, to leave The Fool in a group of one card and form another group with the remaining twenty-one cards. This way, it is possible to break down this second group into three sets of seven cards each. This arrangement is known as the distribution in septenaries and can be found mentioned in The Tarot of the Magitians by Oswald Wirth (1990a). Although its antiquity predates the date when this author mentions it in 1927, as he refers to this distribution as known and part of the tarot tradition[9].

This distribution into a triad of the cards, where each group is composed of seven cards, has very ancient antecedents and is consistent with the symbolic universe in which the first decks were created. Evidence of this can be found in the magnificent work of Dante Alighieri[10], the Divine Comedy. The author of this work lived in Florence, Italy, at the end of the 13th and beginning of the 14th century, where he wrote this book, which has a complex numerical symbolism in its structure.

The Divine Comedy consists of three parts, that is, a triad: Inferno, Purgatorio, and Paradiso. But the symbolism does not end here, as each of its parts consists of thirty-three cantos, to which if the introductory canto is added, the total comes to 100.

This triadic structure in which it is proposed to order the major arcana is completely consistent with the worldview of the time when the first decks were created. It is equivalent to the concept of the Holy Trinity (Father, Son, and Holy Spirit). From the perspective of numerical symbolism, if this triadic structure is combined with the four suits of the minor arcana[11], we obtain the

9. The contemporary author Phillipe Camoin claims to have originated this structure, but the truth is that it predates him by a significant margin, as can be confirmed in the aforementioned citation from Wirth. To see Camoin's ambitious claims, you can visit his website at https://es.camoin.com/tarot/Presentacion-diagrama-Camoin-es.html.

10. Among the many notable aspects of the poet that we can mention is his membership in the initiatory order seeking knowledge: the Fieles de Amor, and his connection to the Order of the Templars. The mystical order Fieles de Amor, based in Florence, was likely the lay branch of the Order of the Templars. Marsilio Ficino, the Florentine sage, founder of Neoplatonism, and translator of the Corpus Hermeticum, subsequently belonged to this order.

11. In this case, the groups composed of each suit of the minor arcana contain fourteen cards, which is also a multiple of seven.

Illustration 1

number 7, and with this, the arrangement of seven cards in three groups is completed.

To obtain a diagram with this arrangement, the twenty-one cards are placed in three rows, one for each septenary, resulting in a presentation like Illustration 1.

In the first row, at the bottom, we can say the base, is the first septenary, which is composed of the following arcana: The Consultant (The Magician[12]), The Female Consultant (The High Priestess), The Empress, The Emperor, The Master (The Pope), The Two Paths (The Lovers), and The Chariot.

The second septenary is located in the middle row, therefore, in a stage of transition, and groups the arcana: Justice, The Old Man (or The Hermit), The Wheel of Fortune, Strength, The Gib-

____

12. I leave the equivalent name of the arcana in the Tarot of Marseille in parentheses, in case the reader is more familiar with this denomination.

bet (The Hanged Man), arcana XIII[13], and Temperance.

The third septenary is located in the third or top row, therefore, in a moment of realizations, and contains the following arcana: Aker (or The Devil), The Tower, The Star, The Moon, The Sun, The Cycle (or Judgment), and The World.

We can see this triadic structure displayed, without the figure of The Fool, in Illustration 1.

---

13. Although this card is popularly known as The Death due to the figure represented on it, it is unnamed and only has the number XIII for identification.

Themes of the Septenaries

In general terms, we can say that the central motif or theme of each of the septenaries is as follows[14]:

• First septenary: from The Magician to The Chariot, the motifs represent people, figures of power, or referents. Generally, this group of cards alludes to the human sphere, the motifs are characters that had a real existence at the time of the creation of the first known decks.

• Second septenary from Justice to Temperance, corresponds to abstract concepts or names: values or virtues that the human being must cultivate, that should regulate society, or on which one must pay attention to avoid stumbling blocks in personal development.

• Third septenary, from The Devil to The World. In this group, the level of abstraction is higher, situating the perspective of the human being in the cosmic environment and the cycles they go through, in a long-term view, and ends with an emphasis on spiritual realization in the card The World.

The recently described scheme proposes a comprehensive structure of the arcana that expands and enriches its broad symbolism, as classifying the major arcana into three septenaries and The Fool allows each card to be considered in the theme grouping each septenary, rather than considering it in isolation. This places it in a scenario where there is a narrative shared with its group. Common challenges and opportunities for each group of cards gathered in a septenary.

On the other hand, the arrangement of the cards in this sche-

---

14. This arrangement into three septenaries, in addition to the mention of Wirth that I cited earlier, can be found in modern authors who have used it as an accurate explanatory model of the tarot structure. These approaches can be seen in (Rodes & Sanchez, 2014) and (Bozzelli, 2014), among others.

me allows them to be related in a somewhat more complex way than simply relating to the ones next to them, and we can extend their links to those that are above, below, or diagonally, as these related cards will perform a similar function at another stage of development.

For example, in the first septenary, if we examine arcana III and IIII, we can see that The Empress is followed by The Emperor, and the latter directs his gaze towards The Empress, whereas she does not act reciprocally but instead looks straight ahead.

Another example illustrating these relationships, which we will see in more detail in the following chapters, is the relationship between arcana VI, XIII, and XX. These three cards are located in the penultimate position of their row, one above the other in the first, second, and third septenary, respectively. In this arrangement, we can make the following generic reflection: The Two Paths (VI) represents a decision, so if we make a choice, it will lead to a change (arcana XIII), which will eventually conclude in a judgment or evaluation in The Cycle (XX).

The three septenaries offer a model of analysis in which it is possible to establish relationships like these and others more complex. Later, I will examine some of the main ones, leaving in the hands of the reader a powerful tool with which to let their imagination fly.

GET Structure

In the Tarot of Marseille and most decks, there is a structure that is implicit in the distribution of the cards, and in some cases, the experienced tarotist becomes familiar with it and gradually begins to use it in their readings. In the preceding section, we have examined the configuration that is common to this type of decks.

However, the GET adds an additional organization that complements this structure. In the following lines, we will see these additional elements that characterize the deck of Maritxu Guler.

The GET proposes its own structure, which is synthesized in two images: on the back or reverse of the cards and in the figure of The Consultant.

The first represents a seven-pointed star, with the symbols of the seven known planets in antiquity[15] drawn at each of its points, and the second, the figure of a male human being, with the same seven planets, drawn on his body, connected by a spiral.

Before continuing, I want to make an epistemological clarification. This proposition about the structure of the GET is a theory for which I take responsibility as an observer, since none of the creators of the deck makes an explicit reference to this interpretation. However, I consider that this way of approaching the GET is consistent with its symbolism, underlies its entire structure, and provides considerable interpretive richness.

Having said that, let's examine the mentioned figures:

The star on the back of the cards

As mentioned, the back of the cards contains a seven-pointed star, inscribed in a circle. This figure is similar to the five-poin-

---

15. Or planets in astrology. The distinction is necessary because the Moon and the Sun are not strictly planets according to the definition of modern astronomy.

ted star inscribed in a circle that inevitably reminds us of the image of Vitruvian Man popularized by Leonardo da Vinci. In turn, this star contains at each of its ends the symbol of a planet. From above and in a counterclockwise direction, we have: the Sun, Venus, Mercury, the Moon, Saturn, Jupiter, and Mars.

The way the star is drawn offers two possibilities of arrangement, each with two respective modalities.

The first is to follow a circular direction as I did previously, that is, counterclockwise. The other possibility is to rotate in the opposite direction, like the hands of a clock. In this case, starting with the Sun, I would have followed with Mars, Jupiter, Saturn, the Moon, Mercury, and reached Venus to complete the tour of the seven planets.

Illustration 2

The other option for arrangement is to consider that the star is drawn continuously, without lifting the hand, therefore, if we start with the Sun, it is followed by the Moon and then: Mars, Mercury, Jupiter, Venus to end with Saturn, in this way of traversing it.In this modality, the other direction of arrangement is to start with the Sun again, continue with Saturn, and then

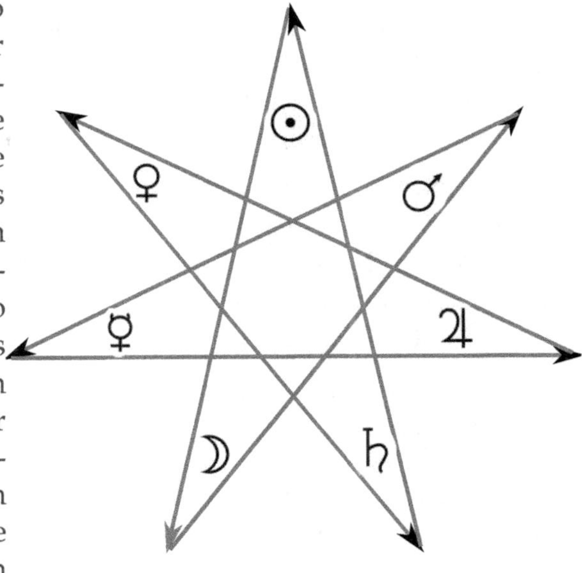

Illustration 3
37

follow with: Venus, Jupiter, Mercury, Mars, and end with the Moon.

This star and its association with astrological symbolism have an extensive presence in the European tradition and are closely related to alchemical symbolism, as we can see in this image where the symbolism of VITRIOL[16] is incorporated.

The symbolism of this image is complex, and its complete analysis goes beyond the scope of this work. For the purposes of our interest in this study, it is worth noting that the image features a seven-pointed star inscribed within a double circle, with the seven planets at each of its points, in the reverse order to that presented by Maritxu Guler on the back of the GET cards. In the image, additional symbols

Illustration 4

are found on the sides and behind the circle. Two hands, one of them holding a torch on the left side of the image, representing the element fire, and the other a bladder, on the right, representing the element air. Below the frame, there are two feet, one in water and the other on land. In this way, the four extremities complete the symbolism, adding the four elements.

Additionally, on each side of this image, there is a man and a woman crowned with the symbols of the sun and the moon on their heads, which refers to the concept of duality, opposition, and complementarity, through the man and the woman.

This symbol was represented in various forms during the Middle Ages (Arndt, 2004), and its overall meaning alludes to a metaphor of creation and spiritual transcendence as illustrated by

---

16. From the Latin acronym "Visita Interiora Terrae Rectificando Invenies Occultum Lapidem," which in English can be translated as: "Search within the earth and by rectifying, you will find the secret stone."

the acronym VITRIOL (Arndt, 2004), which refers to the creative force. On the other hand, the sequence of the planets suggests a metaphor for the evolution of different aspects of the person, as we will see later when we apply these concepts to tarot readings.

We can consider the guide proposed by the seven-pointed star on the back of the cards as a celestial map and therefore, oriented towards the transcendent issues of a reading.

The Consultant: The Map Inscribed in the Body

The general scheme or structure of the GET is completed when, in addition to the image of the star on the back, card number I, The Consultant, is incorporated.In this triumph, Maritxu Guler deviates from the usual tradition that depicts the first arcana as a conjurer before a table, on which all the elements with which he will perform his act are displayed. Respecting the sense of the symbolism of the arcana that shows a character in a creative act, the author of the deck presents a human being covered with a loincloth and the figures of the planets inscribed on his body connected by a spiral, starting from the heart and ending at the forehead.

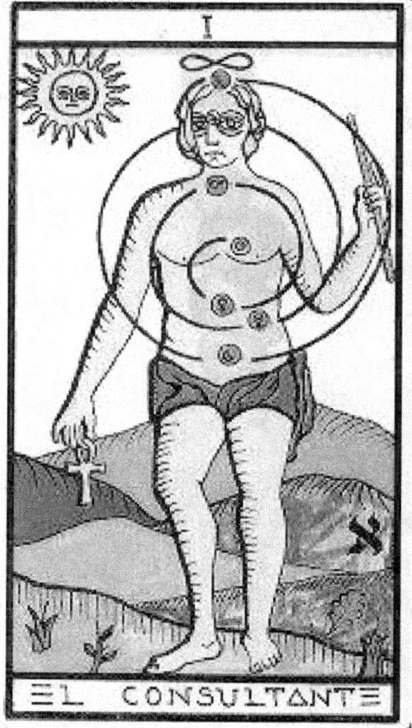

Illustration 5

The symbolism of the semi-nude figure indicates that the creative work's main object is the individual himself and coincides with some initiatory orders where the applicant is stripped of his traditional clothes and presents himself with minimal attire.

Again, if we consider the guide proposed in this card, with the seven planets inscribed on a human body, we can see that the previous celestial guide has now become embodied, and therefore, in this case, alludes to mundane or earthly matters and can be used for the interpretation of this order of things in reading and interpretation.

The image is very expressive and speaks for itself. For years

I used it in different readings I did with this deck, however, its origin remained hidden to me for years, until I accidentally stumbled upon a copy of the book Practical Theosophy (2003) by the 17th-century Christian mystic Johann Geog Gichtel[17], which includes several images of a human being, with what appears to be the first representation in the West of the chakra system used in Hinduism[18].

This image not only has a great similarity in its features and physiognomy with The Consultant of Maritxu Guler but also the posture is equivalent. His left hand points upward with the index finger and the right directs its palm toward the earth. His feet are in a square, with his heels forming a vertex and the left foot pointing forward, with the right retracted, being the support, thus, the character has the characteristic posture of The Magician of the Tarot of Marseille and also of some initiatory orders.

But this similarity does not stop there, the character also has the symbols of the seven planets at the locations of the chakras, just as they

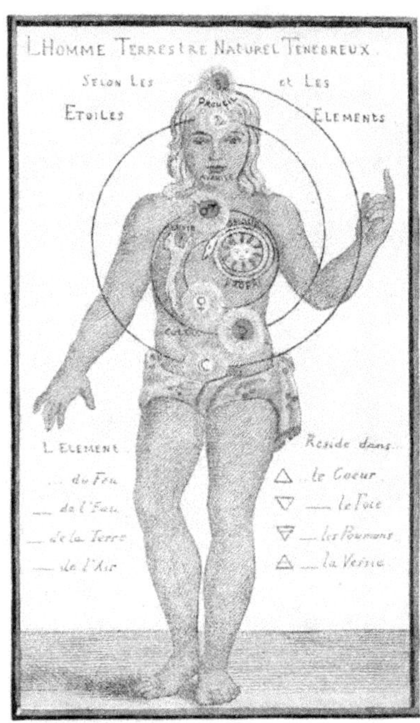

Illustration 6

are found in The Consultant, and not only that, but also the symbols of the planets are connected by the same spiral.

As can be seen, the similarity is astonishing and it is most likely that Gichtel's figure[19] was the source of inspiration for the crea-

____

17. Part of Gichtel's works are based on the Works of Jacob Böhme, third volume.

18. In Hinduism and other Indian traditions such as Tantrism, chakras are energy centers located in specific areas of the body, within a subtle and energetic conception of human physiology.

19. It is not the subject of this book, but the sources for Gichtel's images can be traced further back in history. Gichtel was a theosophist and,

tors of The Consultant of the GET.

---

as a follower of this doctrine, he was familiar with the works of Jacob
Böheme, in which some illustrations similar to his can be found.

GET Navigation Chart: A Seven-Pointed Star

Now that we understand the origins or at least the source of inspiration for the images on the back of the cards and The Consultant, we can relate them to form a powerful system that gives sense and structure to the deck in general terms.

To explain this, I will refer to a scheme of the cards that is implicit in the deck and not described in the material provided by Maritxu Guler in her instruction booklet or in any other source I know of. Somehow, knowing this scheme and its utility has been the fruit of my experience with the deck and the research it has forced me to conduct to

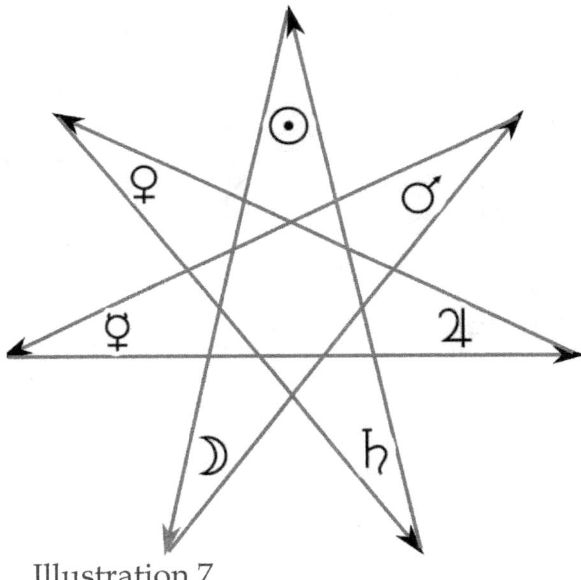

Illustration 7

understand it in depth. I hope this tool will be useful for others interested in tarot reading as it has been for me. In my early days with the cards, I turned to this guide in a utilitarian, almost accidental way, because I needed something that would serve as a "memory aid" for the properties I assigned to the positions of the cards surrounding the one selected by a consultant.

For this purpose, I used the star on the back of the cards to arrange the cards in the spread. Starting the construction of this from the position of the Sun at the top of the star and following the sequence suggested by the arrows, I placed the cards at each of the following points of the arrow, with the main card of the

43

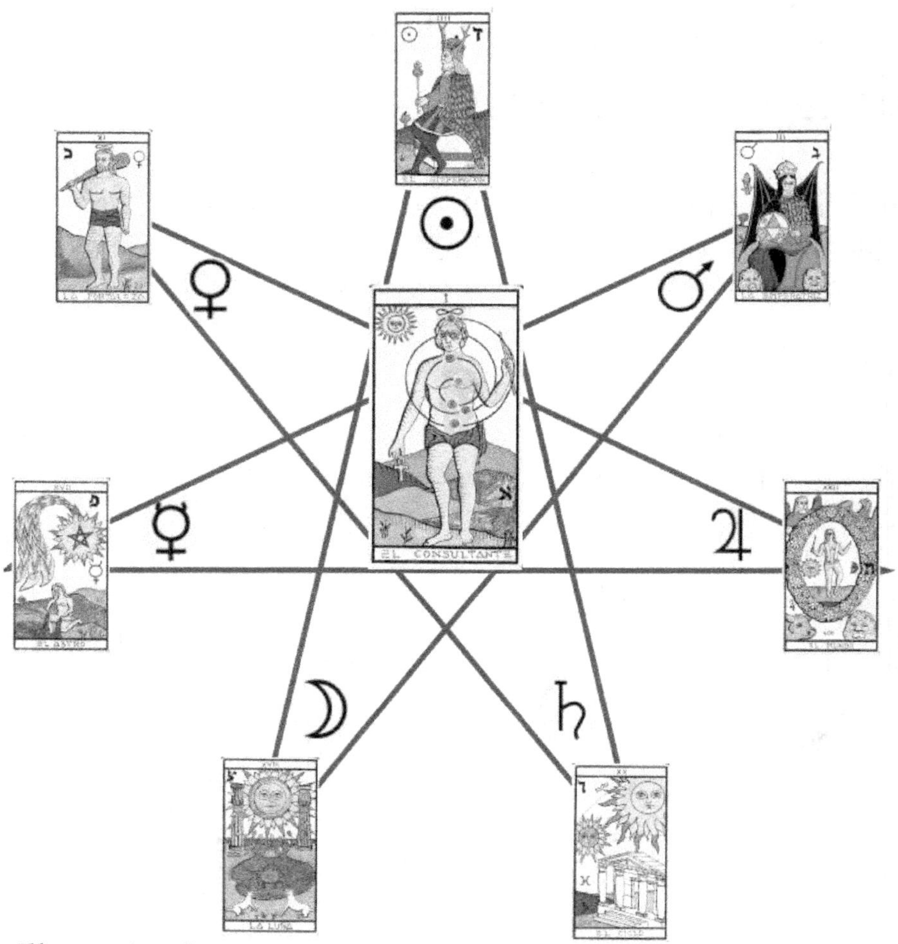

Illustration 8

spread located in the central position of the star. In this way, I began to use eight cards in a reading: the central card chosen by the consultant and seven cards, one at each point of the star.

The scheme followed for this spread is shown in Illustration 7, without the arrangement of the cards.Once the complementary cards and the main card of the spread are arranged in the same position as the star on the back of the deck, I assigned to each of these positions the properties attributed to the planets located in that position.

That is, in Illustration 8, in which the seven major arcana are

44

randomly arranged as an example, The Consultant occupies the central position, and The Emperor is in the place of the Sun, with which, the symbolism of this card can be combined with the properties of said planet.

Following a clockwise direction, The Empress is located in the position of Mars and so on until completing the full turn with Strength, which is located in the upper left position where the planet Venus is.

On the other hand, if we examine the arrangement of the cards in Illustration 8 and relate it to the figure of card number I, The Consultant, we can link the cards by guiding ourselves by the location of the planets on the body of the figure.

For example, The Moon is located at the point of the star which, coincidentally in this case, corresponds to the Moon. If we transfer this arrangement to the body in the figure of arcana number I, we can see that the Moon is located at the position of the chakra approximately where the uterus is in a woman or the prostate in a man.

The purpose of this chapter is to present the general structure implicit in the GET, so I will not go into further detail, in order not to lose sight of the overall perspective of the deck's structure. I will examine this spread more closely in a section specifically dedicated to this topic. What I want to highlight from these two images: The Consultant and the back of the cards, is that they provide a powerful guide for articulating the deck as a whole.

The image on the back of the cards, with its abstract, almost purely geometric symbolism, offers a guide for the social and transcendent aspects related to the context of the query, through the characteristics associated with each planet.

In astrology, it is understood that these seven planets are both personal and social at the same time. They are personal because they allude with their characteristics to basic human impulses, to aspects that characterize us in our inner self. At the same time, they are social, because their symbolism corresponds to the transition or the link we establish with our environment, particularly the relationships we establish with those around us and with whom we interact.

I know that at this point, the skeptical reader of astrology will turn up their nose and flip the page, discounting this understanding of the deck. But the proposed system should not be reduced to astrology and in my opinion is independent of it, as its essence lies in the characterology or taxonomy performed on the different aspects of human activities. This classification of human personality is very useful when it is necessary to simplify economically the immense variety and emotional richness that people can present.

The authors, Maritxu Guler and Luis Peña Longa, use the symbolism present in the astrological tradition[20], since it corresponds to the tradition codified for centuries in tarot decks, but abstracting from this aspect, it is possible to make equivalent the taxonomy of the seven planets to other similar systems such as the Enneagram or characterologies of psychology, such as: Kretschmer's typology[21], Raymond Cattell's 16 personality factors[22], or the classification of people into visual, auditory, and kinesthetic types of Neuro-Linguistic Programming.

Just as the back of the cards, with the star and planets, can be seen in a social dimension, the arrangement of the planets on the body of The Consultant allows the incorporation of the personal aspect in the interpretation and uses this arrangement as a guide

20.   For this purpose, they rely on the existing correspondence between the letters of the Hebrew alphabet and the signs of the zodiac, along with the celestial bodies known in astrology.

21.   Kretschmer's typology is one of the earliest classifications to appear in this field and sought to group people according to their physical characteristics, linking them with personality traits. This theory classifies individuals into three main groups: pyknic, asthenic (or leptosomatic), and athletic. It proposes a fourth group, dysplastic, in which atypical individuals are assigned.

22.   Cattell's theory groups the characteristics of different types of people into 16 factors, and each of these is a continuum between two poles. For example, Affectivity, which ranges from Schizothymia (low affectivity) to Cyclothymia (high affectivity), or Reasoning, which can be either High Intelligence or Low Intelligence. See the Cattell 16 Personality Factor Test (16 PF) at https://psicologiaymente.com/personalidad/test-personalidad-16-factores-cattell-pf, accessed on October 17, 2018.

or reading map for internal issues of personal development or even health in relation to the question guiding the reading.

The way a deck is organized gives us a global vision of its main characteristics. Familiarizing oneself with this is one of the first steps that an advanced student should take to start making the most of their tarot. This advancement should continue with the understanding of the symbolic systems that accompany the deck.

Symbolic Systems of the GET

In general, tarot decks are based around symbolic systems, and any version of tarot, such as the Tarot of Marseille or the Waite-Smith[23] Tarot, has several symbolic systems that act complementarily and on different levels as tools for reading and interpretation.

These symbolic systems function like layers, which can be delved into as we become familiar with the knowledge of the tarot.

Layered knowledge allows someone approaching a deck to start interacting with it after a short period of training. In-depth knowledge of the entire set of symbolic systems included in the tarot is not necessary to make it a useful tool for self-reflection and understanding others, as preliminary knowledge will enable fruitful practice with the cards.

These layers of knowledge are not rigid; it is not necessary to exhaustively understand one symbolic system to access another, as these layers sometimes overlap, and information on one level may allow access and interaction with information on another level.

However, the best way to advance in the knowledge of the tarot is systematically and orderly, but this layering, similar to a hologram[24], allows access to its different levels of knowledge, as they all interact as a harmonious whole.

Certainly, complete knowledge of all the keys incorporated in the deck we are using will give us a more comprehensive, overall

23. This deck is popularly known as the Rider or Rider-Waite Tarot, but its creators are Arthur Edward Waite and his disciple Pamela Colman Smith, so a more appropriate name would be the Waite-Smith Tarot. This is the name I use for this deck since the Rider Company only acts as the printer. Referring to this deck by its popular name would be equivalent to calling the GET Tarot the "Fournier-Guler" Tarot.

24. Holographic objects have the unique property that each of their components can reflect the whole or totality. The term comes from Greek, where 'holos' means all or totality, and 'grama' or 'graphia' means writing or representation. The sense in which I have used the expression is precisely that: a graphic representation of the totality.

view when conducting a reading, and we will be able to access different elements of these to enrich the reading.

In summary, to give an overview, the main symbolic systems contained in the GET, which we can mention are:

Symbol or Theme

The symbol, theme, or motif corresponds to the central idea presented by a card. The card proposes an argument like in a kind of script or narrative, and stringing together several cards allows for storytelling. The central theme of each card is associated with mythological, religious motifs, or reflects the worldview or society in which the first decks were created.

For example, in arcana number XI, Strength of the Tarot of Marseille, it is associated with Hercules' first labor, the defeat of the Nemean lion, or the hero Gilgamesh who gently holds a lion against his chest.

Numerical Key

The numerical key of the cards is associated with numerology, which aims to systematize and abstract the relationships that exist in nature and from this, establishes a mystical relationship between numbers, living beings, and physical or spiritual forces.

From the properties associated with numbers, particularly those that constantly appear in our lives, regularities emerge, which are used as a basis to guide us based on our strengths and aspects we need to enhance.

This theory, as far as we know, has its origin in ancient Greece[25], being authored by Pythagoras and later disseminated by Plato and Aristotle.

In 530 BC, Pythagoras, a Greek philosopher, methodically developed a relationship between numbers and music from the relationship between the length of a string and musical notes. This discovery allowed for a quantitative and numerical conceptualization of music and is an example of the regularities in nature that can be represented through numbers.

Pythagoras extended his theory to the relationship between the distances of planets and their "numerical vibration." He named this theory the "music of the spheres." Through his numerological method, he asserted that words have a sound that vibrates in consonance with the frequency of numbers as another facet of the harmony of the universe and the laws of nature.

As tarot cards are associated with numbers, relationships can be established based on these numbers, derived from the properties associated with the numbers. For example, the previously mentioned arcana XI, which has a high and therefore complex number, can be numerologically reduced to 2, the result of adding the numerals 1 and 1 that compose it, from which the arcana number II is obtained, The High Priestess in the GET, a feminine figure associated with gentleness.

Astrological Key

In tarot decks, it is possible to establish a correspondence between the cards and astrology, linking the cards (mainly Major Arcana) and astrological symbolism. Usually, this relationship is implicit in the cards, and only the expert, after a thorough study of astrology and its correspondence with the cards, can use this knowledge in tarot reading.

---

25. It is very likely that Pythagoras and Greek culture in general drew from the wellsprings of Egyptian and Babylonian knowledge, as these civilizations had developed mathematics and numerical symbolism centuries earlier, and the Greeks maintained rich exchanges with these cultures. However, this does not mean that the Greek route was not the means by which this knowledge was transmitted to the West.

In the GET, this correspondence is explicit, and the major arcana include the twelve astrological signs and the seven planets of astrology. In some of the cards, more than one astrological sign can be found, as in the case of The Star, and in others, none, such as The Fool and arcana number XIII.

In the case of Temperance, here it is associated with the sign Scorpio, which is drawn at the bottom right above the number 50.

Maritxu Guler used as a source for this association the correspondences established by Eliphas Levi between the zodiac signs and the Major Arcana.

Color Key

All decks follow a color scheme that characterizes them. This particularly distinguished the earliest known decks, which were hand-painted. Later, when plates began to be used for mass reproduction of the cards, the decks lost richness, as only basic colors were used in their printing. This is what Jodorowsky, for example, has argued in his proposal for the restoration of the Tarot of Marseille, to what he claims was its original color line.

On the other hand, a well-designed deck has the ability to support the central motif of each arcana through subtle color cues. For instance, arcana number VI, The Two Paths in the GET, generally represents a decision and is

usually associated with a choice in the realm of feelings. This motif is expressed with a legend from Greek mythology: the choice of Hercules. Before embarking on his famous twelve labors, the hero must choose the path he will follow for his endeavors: virtue or pleasure.

To represent this story, the card shows a man accompanied by two women, each appearing to sway him to their side. In some decks, these women are clearly distinguished by their age: one young and the other mature. In the GET, this age distinction is also possible, as one of the women has long hair, associated with feminine youth, and the other has short hair, a sign of maturity. However, it is distinctive in this card that one of the women is dressed in red (pleasure) and the other in a blue dress (virtue).

Thus, in a deck, the color line expresses and reinforces the symbolic aspects of each card and gives a sense of overall unity to the work.

Sacred Geometry

Just as numbers are used to abstractly represent relationships that exist in nature, geometric shapes are used to express them. The level of abstraction is deep enough to formulate an entire cosmogony that explains the generation of dimensional space. In the words of Oswald Wirth, referring to the creative process and mentioning the number 1: "...he is the mathematical point of no dimension, but whose movement brings about all geometric shapes.He is the subjective centre around which objectivity is conceived."[26] (Wirth, 1990a, p. 159)

As a reference, let's note that from the symbolism of the dot · (the unmanifested); the cross + (the manifested or binary); the triangle Δ (material manifestation and the simplest geometric shape); and the square □ (the quaternary, associated with the four elements), this complete language of symbolic forms is developed. Sometimes, these representations are multiple, and for example, the cross can also represent the material with its four ends.

26.   Based on the English version.

The point representing no-thingness, the moment before the existence of the world, or as we would say in modern language, the moment prior to the "big bang," is the essential concept around which space is constructed. A projected point creates a line, a one-dimensional figure.

In the same way, from the projection of a line in space, a square is created, and with it, we obtain a rectangular figure that already has two dimensions. This symbolism is equivalent to the intersection of two lines (as in the cross).

Lastly, by projecting a point upward on a triangle (the simplest two-dimensional figure), we obtain a triangular pyramid or tetrahedron, which is also the simplest solid. This solid is three-dimensional and exists in the space in which we are accustomed to operating.

The previously mentioned process creates basic forms which are symbolized by the point or circle, the cross, the triangle, and the square. These basic forms can be combined with each other to generate more complex shapes.

In turn, these four elements are associated with metaphysical concepts that are summarized as follows:

Geometric Shape	Meaning
Point, Circle	Nothingness when it is a point, or the whole in its circular form. Generally: the immaterial, the spiritual.
Line	The duality expressed by the ends of the line. This concept has a dual meaning, on one hand complementarity and on the other, opposition
Triangle	As it is the overcoming of duality, of change, it represents balance. It is the synthesis, the child in the couple.
Square	The world of the material, the earthly, the concrete, the four elements.

The symbolic language of geometry is present in every tarot deck and expresses content through its symbolism, also reinforcing the central content of the card.

As we can see in the figure of The Emperor card, the central character is the temporal ruler in the world of men, that is, of the material. His figure expresses this idea through the cloak that covers him, the crown that encircles him, and the scepter he holds in his hand.

This concept is subtly reinforced by some aspects related to symbolic geometry:

• The cross formed by his crossed legs.

• Because in the scepter, the cross (the material) is above a sphere (a circle), the immaterial.

• The seat on which he rests is not a typical throne, but an object similar to a cube, again associated with the number four, therefore, with the material.

It should be noted that in geometric symbolism, Maritxu Guler rigorously follows the symbolism of the classic decks most closely adhering to tradition.

Kabbalistic Key

This pattern of interpretation is linked to the tree of life in Kabbalah and is probably one of the central aspects of tarot symbolism. In traditional decks, like the Tarot of Marseille, this aspect is implicit and only the most knowledgeable can make use of all the possibilities offered by Kabbalistic tradition, even though all tarot readers indirectly benefit from the complex set of relationships incorporated in Kabbalistic understanding.

According to recent research, Jewish mysticism in the Iberian Peninsula developed a philosophical and symbolic synthesis around Kabbalah that contributed to the formation of the tarot deck. This contribution from Spain, combined with Catharism from southern France and the input of researchers from nor-

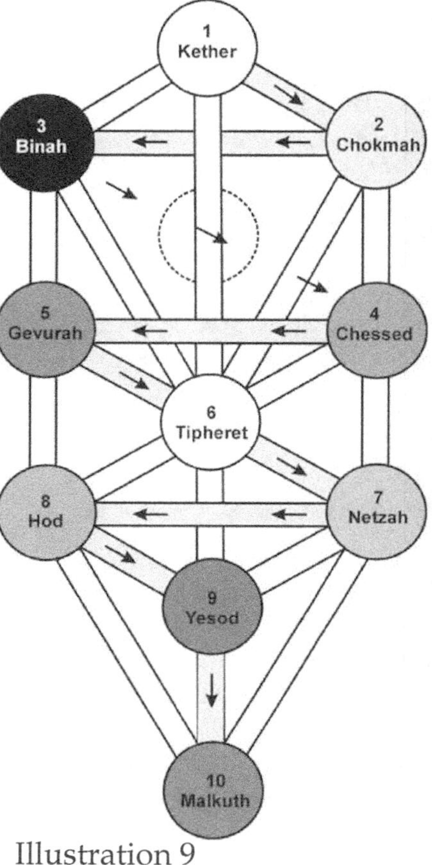

Illustration 9

thern Italy like Pico della Mirandola, in an amalgam that crystallized in the secret societies of the time and ended up reflected in the Tarot[27].

The cultural environment in the Iberian Peninsula was rich and

27. Delving further into this point would divert us from the central theme of the book, which is not to say that it is a matter of no interest. On the contrary, understanding the sources from which the tarot originates aids in its comprehension and use. For those interested in exploring this topic further, I recommend the excellent work of Christine Payne-Towler, such as "Foundation of the Esoteric Tradition. Tarot of the Holy Light" (2016)

open thanks to the atmosphere of tolerance developed by the Arab rulers from approximately 700 to 1500 AD. During this long period, Al-Andalus developed a policy of cultural flourishing in which the three religions of the book (Judaism, Christianity, and Islam) could coexist in an atmosphere of mutual enrichment. In this context, Jewish mysticism developed a special form of "technology" for transcendence in the Iberian Peninsula, known as Kabbalah.

Jewish mysticism synthesizes its tradition in a figure called The Tree of Life, which connects through twenty-two paths, ten sefirot (or centers) that comprise it. This scheme reflects a cosmogony, inspired by the biblical Genesis, in which divinity at the moment before creation manifests in the first sefirah Kether and then, through successive manifestations, travels the path indicated by the arrows in Illustration 9, until ending in the tenth sefirah, Malkuth, the kingdom, which corresponds to the world of human beings.

In this sense, Kabbalah, in addition to being a cosmogony, is also a representation of The Fall as presented in Genesis, from Adam and Eve's expulsion from Paradise, and at the same time, as the paths represent not only a unidirectional journey, it serves as a guide for transcendence and return to divinity.

As noted, the contribution of Jewish mysticism in shaping the tarot towards the end of the Middle Ages was significant and may have defined the definitive number of Major Arcana to align with the twenty-two letters of the Hebrew alphabet. The incorporation of this key gave the early decks the stable form in which they have reached us today. But not only that, it also offers a key to establishing astro-alphanumeric correspondences[28] that connect with traditional symbolism.

These correspondences have been implicit in tarot decks since they took their definitive form with 22 major arcana, but they

---

28. With this formulation of the tarot, the astrological knowledge of antiquity, the numerical correspondences, and the 22 letters of the Hebrew alphabet were synthesized in the same way that Christine Payne-Towler (2016) uses them.

have not always been explicitly shown. Maritxu Guler's deck does this by relating each card of the Major Arcana to a letter of the Hebrew alphabet.

But it does not only make this relationship; it also adopts a set of correspondences predating Christian influence in Kabbalah that exactly matches the Jewish equivalencies as established in the Sefer Yetzirah (Kaplan, 1997).

According to Christine Payne-Towler, the GET is the first deck to print these correspondences explicitly: "So, once again, history tells us that the roots of this pattern are considerably older than any other, although Marixtu Erlanz de Guler, author of The Great Esoteric Tarot, was the first to print them on a Tarot deck" (Payne-Towler, 2016).

Alchemical Key

As anyone who has explored this form of knowledge with transcendent interest knows, alchemy has two planes of development: one in which the alchemist performs transformations with elements and compounds in a way very similar to what modern chemistry[29] is, and the other, oriented towards the inner transformation of the person, to make them a better individual and with the ultimate goal of achieving spiritual realization, however that may be understood.

This latter way of understanding and practicing alchemy developed an extraordinary level of secrecy, and its knowledge was transmitted in a reserved manner, largely expressed orally and through symbols and metaphors, so that the essence of the knowledge remained hidden from the uninitiated. The collection of alchemical symbols is part of the European cultural heritage and is closely linked to the people and secret societies that contributed to giving the Tarot its canonical form, thus, its symbolism could not be absent in the cards that make it up.

Several of the arcana allude to the internal transformation to which alchemy appeals, and in the cards, we can find images that

---

29. With the corresponding technical differences specific to each era.

express ideas about initiatory death and its respective rebirth or the completion of the feminine and masculine aspects in the human being.

To illustrate this point, let's mention what O. Wirth says in "The Tarot of the Medieval Imagers" when referring to card number XIII:

> "When you have given everything, you will be reduced to the state of a walking skeleton. You will be as dead, and they will say: flesh has left the bones. Reaping the illusions of the past you will then prepare the land for the future harvests. In the heart of sepulchral darkness the Philosophical Child known as the Son of Putrefaction will take birth" (Wirth, 1990a)[30].

As we see in the text, Oswald Wirth uses metaphorical language to refer to an inner transformation of profound repercussions, which due to its implications can be compared to death. In fact, in psychological terms, it is equivalent to the death or dissolution of the ego, so that the individual is no longer the same.

This alchemical interpretation, which in arcana number XIII is accessible with some basic knowledge on the subject, is also found in the other arcana of the GET and will be shared with the reader as we analyze each one of them.

---

30. The text was originally written in French, and the translation into English is not the best, but it was the only one available.

Septenary Arrangement

One of the merits of tarot decks is their rich logical and relational complexity. At first glance, during our initial encounters with a deck, we only see cards arranged in what seems like a chaotic manner, and this is not necessarily due to our lack of knowledge about the cards. We could perfectly understand their meanings and yet they might still seem disconnected.

Only in subsequent sessions do we begin to see the first relationships, and later, with in-depth study, we start to appreciate the enormous complexity, supported by subtle and powerful logic.

The cards relate to each other through keys and numerical sequences that are supported by the motifs and titles of the cards. Thanks to this, anyone can master complex logical-mathematical relationships in service of a narrative.

In the following lines, I will present schematically one of the "arrangements" that facilitate the understanding of tarot, known as the septenary ordering.

As mentioned earlier, if we consider only the major arcana and leave The Fool in one group and the other twenty-one cards in another, we can arrange this second set into three groups of seven cards each, which I will call septenaries.

The interpretive resource that arises from grouping the arcana into septenaries allows us to attribute common properties or areas of interest for each of the three septenaries.

Firstly, this arrangement into three groups of seven cards (excluding The Fool) allows us to have an overview, making it easier to see relationships between the cards and, above all, the general development or sequence. Following (Rodes & Sanchez, 2014)□ in a synthesized form, these three groups of cards represent or are associated with the following aspects:

From card 1 to 7, that is, from The Magician to The Chariot, the cards indicate names of people or things: they define something known, found in the immediate environment of people. They are persons one could encounter in everyday life or in the institutions of the concrete world. Most of them refer to characters that existed at the time the first decks were created.

From cards 8 to 14, that is, from Justice to Temperance, appear abstract names: virtues and laws that the human being must understand, the world of reason, and achievements.

From cards 15 to 21, that is, from The Devil to The World, the names of the cards correspond to cosmic forces: the figures are smaller, and special importance is given to the sky, to the world of the spirit.

In the first septenary, the cards at the extremes and the center (The Magician, The Emperor, and The Chariot) are male figures. This septenary, corresponding to the initial one, represents the creative principle.

In the second septenary, the equivalent cards at the extremes and the center (Justice, Strength, and Temperance) are female.

This follows the ternary structure characteristic of esoteric symbolism, and therefore, this septenary symbolizes the feminine principle, the receptive, the dual.

In the third septenary, the cards at the extremes and the middle (The Devil, The Moon, and The World) feature both sexes, indicating that here the synthesis of the two previous stages is realized. In this septenary, the themes proposed by the cards correspond to abstract principles, of a celestial or transcendent order.

The association of the septenaries with three principles: the first being creative, the second receptive, and the third the synthesis; is already anticipated by the first three cards of the Tarot. The first, The Magician, is male, the second, The High Priestess, is female, and the third, The Empress, is pregnant[31], containing two beings within her – herself and her child.

This brief introduction to the structuring of the Major Arcana into three septenaries and The Fool aims to present the frameworks that I will follow to expound the main cards of a tarot deck. I hope that this scheme allows those who are new to the study of tarot to access a tool that helps them familiarize themselves with the cards.

---

31. According to the traditional symbolic interpretation.

Major Arcana

In a tarot deck, the Major Arcana constitute the essential aspect. The cards that make it up are images of different events in the earthly lives of human beings and of transcendent aspects that occupy their concerns and interests.

The Major Arcana, in the version standardized in decks like the Marseille, consist of 22 cards, which through their images represent stories, themes, or motifs full of symbolism.

As I pointed out in the introductory section to the Symbolic Systems of the GET, the keys of an arcana are expressed in several layers with different levels of depth, interacting with each other. In a reading, each arcana will express those aspects that are relevant in that interpretation. This will depend on the interaction with the other cards involved in the spread and the interaction between the consultant and the tarot reader with the cards.

In an arcana, these layers of symbolic systems add threads to the card, and the reading pulls one or several of them, so following the path proposed by one of these serves as a guide to navigate through the interpretation.

This does not mean that the meaning of a card is arbitrary, but rather that it is constructed in context, in interactions with other cards. Therefore, those beginning in the world of tarot should be wary of dogmatic definitions, which, unfortunately, are abundant in beginner's manuals available in the market.

This interactive and dynamic aspect of the cards, where the meaning of one is constructed by relating to others, gives a systemic value to tarot: the cards have certain value as they relate to other cards.

In this sense, each triumph, or Major Arcana, tells a story, but the additional value of each card is that the story it encloses is a narrative that in turn constructs stories in interaction with other arcana, and these stories have the capacity to continue constructing stories ad infinitum.

This constructive capacity of tarot was used by Italo Calvino in a literary exercise in two of his novels: "The Castle of Crossed Destinies" and "The Tavern of Crossed Destinies." In these novels, using the Visconti Tarot and the Marseille Tarot, the writer adds plots that emerge from stories proposed by the cards and that intersect with the main theme.

This creative exercise artistically and practically demonstrates the narrative unfolding that tarot can provide.

The central element in a triumph is the motif or story it seeks to convey, and if the value or meaning we assign to it is appropriate, i.e., it expresses sufficient complexity and malleability, it will account for the traditional and symbolic aspects associated with the arcana. This provides adequate content for the reading.

Major Arcana

In a tarot deck, the Major Arcana are the essential aspect. The cards depict various events from human earthly life and transcendent aspects concerning human worries and interests.

The Major Arcana, as standardized in decks like the Marseille, consist of 22 cards. Through their images, they represent stories or themes rich in symbolism.

As noted in the introduction to the Symbolic Systems of the GET, an arcana's keys are expressed in layers with varying depths, interacting with each other. In a reading, each arcana expresses relevant aspects for that interpretation, depending on its interaction with other cards in the spread and the interaction between the consultant and the tarot reader.

In an arcana, these layers of symbolic systems add depth, and the reading pulls from one or several threads, following the path provided by these guides.

The meaning of a card is not arbitrary but is constructed in context, in interactions with other cards. Thus, beginners in the world of tarot should be wary of dogmatic definitions often found in manuals.

The interactive and dynamic aspect of the cards, where a card's meaning is constructed through relationships with others, gives the tarot systemic value. Each card has value as it relates to other cards.

Each Major Arcana tells a story, and the additional value of each card is that its story constructs more stories in interaction with other arcana, capable of endlessly constructing more narratives.

Italo Calvino used this narrative capacity of tarot in his novels "The Castle of Crossed Destinies" and "The Tavern of Crossed Destinies," using the Visconti Tarot and the Marseille Tarot to add subplots emerging from the card stories.

The central element in a Major Arcana is the motif or story it conveys. The Major Arcana are numbered consecutively from 1 to 21 in Roman numerals, with The Fool being unnumbered or numbered 0 in some decks.

Most Major Arcana have a name, usually displayed at the top or bottom of the card, referring to the central motif. However, Arcanum XIII is unnamed, commonly associated with death.

The GET generally follows the Marseille Tarot canon, with significant variations enriching its symbolism. These changes, made by Maritxu, always respect the original card's meaning.

Thus, in presenting the cards, I will highlight the main differences with the Marseille Tarot. This comparative exercise is a deep understanding tool, as I have personally experienced. Therefore, we will systematically apply this methodological tool in developing and presenting the Major Arcana.

Despite the risk of this essay resembling a typical tarot book with generic card meanings, I will present the Major Arcana with the particularities incorporated by the author. As we will see, almost nothing is random, and even seemingly insignificant details contain rich symbolism or reference a historical fact that aids in understanding the card.

Let's then explore each Major Arcana, attempting to unveil their origin and meaning in this special deck, the GET.

First Septenary

As I previously mentioned, it is useful to group the arcana into septenaries, as this facilitates understanding, especially in the initial stage of familiarizing oneself with the deck.

The first septenary includes The Magician to The Chariot. In this septenary, the motifs represent people, figures of power, or references; the arcana indicate names of people or things, defining something known. In general, this group of cards alludes to the human sphere, with the motifs in most decks being characters who existed at the time of their creation, thereby reflecting the social structure of that era.

Interpretatively, they indicate situations in a preliminary stage, from which future developments can be expected. If following the guide of the septenaries, it's beneficial to check if cards from the other two septenaries are present in a reading. For example, if the card being read is The Magician, the starting card of the first septenary, we should look for Justice from the second septenary and Aker from the third septenary.

The cards of this first septenary correspond to a couple of narratives. These first seven cards correlate with the first seven days of creation according to Genesis 1-2 (Jerusalem Bible, 1972) and can be related to the tasks undertaken by the creator on these

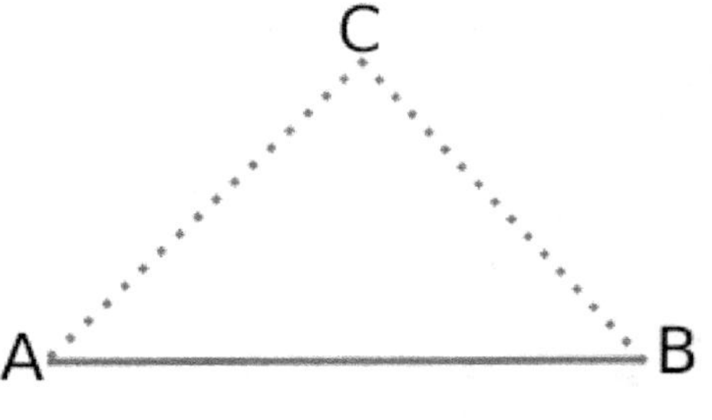

days. Similarly, these arcana can be viewed through the metaphor of constructive geometry. The Fool represents the void, the nothingness, from which the first element emerges: the point (circle), or subjectivity from which all objectivity is constructed, corresponding to The Magician. The projection of the point creates a line, leading to duality, represented in the arcana by The High Priestess.

If the line, represented by the segment AB, projects its own line from each of its ends (A and B) until intersecting with the other projected line, we obtain a triangle (ABC). The corresponding arcana for this is The Empress.

The triangle is the simplest figure and the first to constitute a geometric plane, hence its stability. This is why a three-legged table is always balanced and does not wobble.

Projecting from the ABC plane from its vertices (ABC) to any point (D) results in a triangular-based pyramid (ABCD), the simplest solid in three-dimensional space, the realm of The Emperor.

Transcending the material, mastering the four elements, enables transcendence, the intertemporal, mastery over time, corresponding to The Hierophant.

Having overcome the preliminary challenges, The Fool, who has begun this journey, must make a decision to confirm their will to continue, corresponding to the arcana The Lovers. From a geometric perspective, this is represented by two intersecting triangles, forming a six-pointed star, known as the Star of David or Seal of Solomon.

Finally, if the adventurer has surpassed the initial obstacles and confirmed their decision to proceed, they are in a position to reap success and victory, represented by the card The Chariot. Again, this idea has a geometric representation, through the combination of a square and a triangle, forming a seven-pointed star.

In summary, the cards included in this group are: The Magician, who starts the journey, The High Priestess, who takes the first steps and delves into sensitivity, The Empress, who has achieved the balance of the rational and intuitive, The Emperor, who has gained dominion over the material world through willpower, The Hierophant, who has ascended the spiritual realm and can exercise mastery, The Lovers, representing the need to make decisions about the path to be followed, and The Chariot, indicating that the chosen path in this stage has led to victory.

68

I The Consultant

I have already preliminarily presented this triumph in the GET Structure section. In my opinion, this is one of the cornerstones of the deck, around which innovative ways of laying out the cards in a spread can be built.

In a Marseille deck, this card is named Le Bateleur, literally translating to "one who governs a ship," and by extension, a puppeteer or one who governs the strings. Other authors consider it to represent a magician, which opens a rich universe of interpretive possibilities, as the word magician etymologically shares a root with words like 'may,' 'make,' 'might' in English, or 'macht' in German, all signifying power or action.

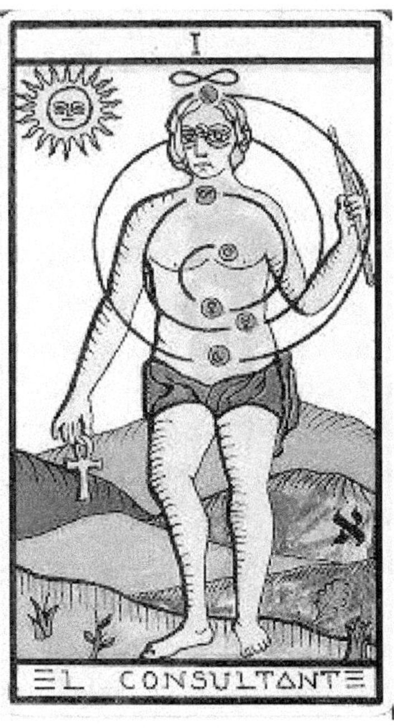

Furthermore, magician is etymologically related to 'magíster' or master. The meaning points to someone capable of doing things, equipped with the abilities and elements to do them. Hence, in the Tarot de Marseille, the character appears standing before a table with at least four elements, associated with the primordial elements: air, water, fire, and earth, which ancient Greek thinkers believed could create everything else.

Another interesting idea about the character's symbolism is that it represents an orchestra or stage director, a figure that directs action in a carnival. This likely stems from the earliest known decks, which, as far as we know today, are from Northern Italy.

The prestidigitator appearing in the card is in a specific body position, generally respected by most Marseille decks and many others. The character, standing, has their right foot retracted and the left foot pointed, forming a square. Their left hand is raised to the sky holding a wand, and the right hand is directed downward, resting on the abdomen and holding a coin or circular figure.

In this card, the Sun is present on the horizon, denoting the creative and fertilizing aspect of this character. Additionally, the associated Hebrew alphabet letter is 'aleph,' indicating will as its main attribute. In the Hebrew alphabet, א 'aleph' is one of the three mother letters, along with מ 'mem' and ש 'shin'; 'aleph' is associated with air[32], while 'mem' and 'shin' are associated with water and fire, respectively.

Despite preliminary differences, which I consider superficial, the figure presented by the GET for this arcana retains the essential characteristics of a Marseille deck, mainly the posture, and adds additional features that, even with fewer elements, incorporate high complexity, which, if not considered, could limit us in interpretation.

As can be seen at first glance, the card lacks the familiar table and objects typically seen on it in traditional tarot decks. However, it includes other elements not present in other decks, such as an intriguing spiral that unfolds from the chest to the head and an ankh cross that the character holds in the right hand.

These two elements replace, and I believe surpass, the objects and table of a traditional tarot, as the primary symbolism of the four elements on the table points to the constructive ability of The Magician, who has a world to create on the journey he begins, and by extension, in that journey, he is also creating himself. In The Consultant of the GET, this reference is explicit; the spiral, the map, is inscribed on the body, hence, there is no transformation without self-transformation.

The semi-nudity of the character reinforces this concept, as he has left behind his usual attire and is ready to embark on his path, leaving behind his old life to become a new man. This nudi-

---

32. Due to its association with the aleph letter of the Hebrew alphabet, the correct relationship of this arcana is with the element of air, according to the correspondence model known as Gra. I mention this point because the presence of the Sun in the card might lead to a misunderstanding regarding its astrological or planetary association.

ty of the character, on the other hand, contributes to the Adamic character that the author seemingly wishes to bestow, especially when associated with the following card, The Consultant, where the figure is completely naked, as Adam and Eve were presumed to be before the Fall.

The object held in the right hand of the character in the figure is an ankh or Egyptian cross, unlike in Marseille decks, where the right hand holds a small circle slightly below the navel. The origin of this symbol, as its name suggests, is from the Egyptian civilization and is also a hieroglyph ('anj') meaning life[33], thus re-affirming the creative and fertility attributes associated with this arcana.

---

33. Another name given to this symbol is the key of life.

II La Consultante

In the Marseille tarot decks, this card is known as "La Papisa" (The High Priestess), and it has sparked numerous controversies in interpretation. By its name, in these decks, it is associated with the fifth arcana, "El Papa" (The Pope), and together with "La Emperatriz" (The Empress) and "El Emperador" (The Emperor), they are part of the earthly court.

Maritxu Guler chose a different approach for this arcana, starting with its name: "La Consultante" (The Consultant), associating it with the first arcana. The differences don't end there but continue with her attire, or rather the lack thereof. In traditional decks, the High Priestess or Papisa is fully clothed, dressed in garments reminiscent of a Mother Superior's habit or the high priestess of a fertility cult.

The explanations for this card are varied since the name it's associated with, "La Papisa," is heretical for the Catholic Church. There are two hypotheses to explain the origin of this card (Méndez Filesi, 2016a). One refers to the legend of Pope Joan, and the other to Manfreda Visconti Pirovano, a distant relative of Filippo Maria Visconti, who was named pope of a heretical sect in Lombardy called the Guglielmites. In both cases, the heretical nature of the character is present, as it represents the possibility of a female figure as the primary authority of the Church.

This heretical nature led to this card being replaced in its symbolism by figures like Juno or Isis to avoid controversy with religious authorities, and this is possibly one of the reasons Maritxu Guler opted for this image.

Essentially, the main symbolism remains preserved in these changes, as the arcana represents fertility in its feminine aspect, elevated to a figure of authority. Although the image moves away from the legend of Pope Joan, Maritxu Guler (1976) explicitly refers to the character of the card as Joan on more than one occasion, as we can see in this comment: "Joan, full of beauty, appears naked. She is between two trees, illuminated by the Moon."

However, pictorially, the GET distances itself from heretical interpretations by presenting us with a young, naked female figure, holding a pomegranate in her right hand and between two trees. The interpretative possibilities offered by this image are varied and rich.

One possibility in the main symbolic theme of the arcana is that the pomegranate, due to the multiplicity of its seeds, represents fertility. Additionally, it allows us to associate the character with Persephone.

According to Greek mythology, Persephone is the daughter of Zeus and Demeter and lived secluded from the other gods with her mother, leading a peaceful life. Demeter was known in the Greek world as the goddess of agriculture, or as a mother goddess or distributor, due to the nourishing nature of the earth. Mother and daughter were associated with the Eleusinian Mysteries, annual initiatory rites in which these two goddesses were principal figures. The importance of these rites in the Greek world led to their extension to the Roman Empire.

Persephone's tranquility with her mother was shattered when Hades, the god of the underworld, abducted her and took her to live with him in his realm. Heartbroken, Demeter searched for her daughter by sea and land without success, finally appealing to Zeus, who pitied Demeter's sorrow. He ordered Hades to release Persephone, but it was stipulated that Persephone must not eat on her return journey. Hades, however, tricked Persephone into eating some pomegranate seeds, six in most versions.

Because of this, Persephone was required to return periodically to the underworld for several months each year[34]. During this

---

34. The number of months that Persephone spends in the underworld

period, the earth is barren, dry, and infertile, but upon her return, vegetation sprouts and blooms, and nature again offers its fruits.

The symbolism proposed for this arcana in the GET has a dual character like Persephone's: barren in the autumn-winter months and fertile in spring-summer. Dual is also the mother-daughter condition in the relationship between Persephone and Demeter, assuming in this triumph the condition of daughter-maiden.

A lateral association with the origins suggested in the previous lines is related to the author's connection with the traditions of the Basque people. The cultural heritage of this region is very special, as many aspects are completely unknown, such as the origin of its language, and it managed to stay outside the cultural penetration of the Roman Empire and the rest of Europe until well into the modern era.

In the religious conceptions of this people, the main figure is Mari, a female deity who resides at the summit of the mountains, usually in their caves. She is typically represented with a woman's body and face and beautiful blonde hair that she combs in the sun with a gold comb. She is the personification of Mother Earth and governs over nature. Of the primitive European mother goddesses, she is the only one who has survived to the present day.

In her role as Mother Earth, Mari is the mother of the Sun and the Moon, and one of her objectives is to restore balance and ensure justice is done. As we can see, many of the characteristics of this deity are appropriate for La Consultante, particularly her golden hair and her relationship with the symbolism of duality, suggesting she may have been a source of inspiration for this card, especially considering that the GET's image is somewhat distanced from what we typically find in Marseille decks.

The dual or even double condition in the symbolism of this arcana is precisely the most suitable for the card that, numerically, is associated with duality. In interpretation, it can be associated

---

in Greek mythology varies depending on the version of the myth and, interestingly, can be influenced by the climate of the region where the story is told

with relationships of attraction and complementarity, as well as opposition and rejection, which will depend on the accompanying cards.

Another possible association of this triumph in the GET is with Eve, Adam's companion and the mother of all humans. The arguments for this option are found, again, in the fruit that the consultante holds in her right hand, equivalent to the fruit with which Adam and Eve were tempted by the serpent. After eating it, they became aware of their nakedness.

Confirming this, the central figure is nude, just as Eve would have been in the Garden of Eden before eating the "forbidden fruit," and also between two trees, recalling the trees of paradise: the tree of knowledge and the tree of life. According to Genesis, by eating the fruit of knowledge, humans become like God, because they gain knowledge of good and evil. Furthermore, the tree of life remains in the Garden of Eden, and if they were to eat from this tree, they would live indefinitely.

This previous interpretation of the triumph brings it closer to El Consultante than to El Papa, as in traditional decks, and reinforces the Adamic character of the first triumph proposed by Maritxu Guler. Thus, the name La Consultante is very appropriate for the second arcana of the deck.

The GET presents La Consultante accompanied by the Moon, indicating that her light is a reflection of the Sun, continuing the idea of duality present in the arcana. The association of this card with the Hebrew alphabet letter corresponds to Beth (ב), a letter whose association corresponds to science. This relationship is supported by the character being between two trees or columns, a symbolic image that inevitably projects us to Solomon's Temple, the quintessential place where science is cultivated.

In more heterodox decks, the second arcana presents a veiled priestess at the entrance of two columns adorned with the letters B and J, which are associated with the columns of the entrance to Solomon's Temple.

As Maritxu Guler (1976) states in her instruction booklet for La Consultante: "She occupies in the structure of the Tarot the place of the door, the passage between the exterior and the interior, the immobile and common point between the house and the street."

III The Empress

From a historical perspective regarding the evolution of the tarot, The Empress has maintained a consistent representation with few exceptions. In the Marseille decks, she is depicted as a female figure of authority and, by her title, as the consort of The Emperor, ruling over the earthly realm.

She is the mature, fertile woman, brimming with vitality and in the prime of her life. To depict this, the authors of the GET portray a woman richly dressed in royal garments, holding the scepter of royalty in her left hand, and what appears to be a shield in her right. Her head is crowned, and two lions lie at her feet. Her back is adorned with two black wings, evoking those of a bat. The context of the card includes a corn cob, associated with the planet Mars and the Hebrew alphabet letter Gimel (ג).

The modifications proposed by Maritxu Guler for this card are minor, largely adhering to the Tarot of Marseille standard. The main variation in the card is found in the object held in her right hand. Traditionally, this is a shield adorned with an imperial eagle. In contrast, the author has chosen an emblem adorned with two triangular (or pyramidal) figures, one dark on top and the other light in color, flanked by the Sun and the crescent Moon[35].

This image, replacing the imperial shield, presents two symbolic elements associated with the card's central theme. On the one hand, the triangles represent the number three, corresponding to the card's number, and on the other, the Sun and Moon remind

---

35. According to how it is visualized in the Northern Hemisphere of the planet.

us that this sovereign rules according to the cycles of nature.

In her clothing, another element links her to the cycles of nature, specifically in her cloak (or short cape), adorned with leaves as if they were feathers.

As noted, she holds an imperial scepter in her right hand, topped with an orb surmounted by a cross. The orb signifies that the empress's reign is earthly, and the cross[36] indicates that her powers are derived from above.

The figure is winged to signify her ascension, echoing the idea of the "Queen of Heaven," a title given to Mary, the mother of Jesus Christ. There's a similar relationship between the Virgin Mary, the maiden, and Mary, the Queen of Heaven, to that between The Consultant (The High Priestess) and The Empress - one a maiden, the other a mature, fertile woman; one Persephone, the other Demeter, both representing two aspects of the same concept.

Maritxu Guler completes the relationship initiated in the previous card, associating it with Persephone. The Consultant (High Priestess) is the daughter or the youthful expression of the woman. The Empress is Demeter, the fully balanced woman, who relates to her daughter in a play of beginning and transcendence, where the latter needs the former, as it is she who sows the seeds, and the former requires the latter to harvest the fruits of what has been sown.

In the corn cob located to the right of the character, Maritxu reinforces the idea of fertility associated with nature, further asserting that The Empress is the representation of the myth of Persephone and her mysteries. If this line of interpretation is followed, The Empress is an expression of The Great Mother or Mother Goddess, a concept prevalent especially in Europe and brought to light by Marija Gimbutas in "The Language of the Go-

---

36. In this specific case, it should be understood in this way, as the symbolism of the cross, in this context, should be more closely associated with an institution like the Church, rather than other interpretations where the symbolism of the cross is related to the number four and the four elements.

ddess" (1996) and other publications. These works have paved the way for a new perspective on the historical role of women, opening up intriguing viewpoints.

According to Gimbutas, prehistoric Europe was home to numerous societies organized with gender equality, where female prominence was evident in all societal aspects, particularly in ritual practices associated with fertility and agriculture.

Evidence of this is found in the images of female figures unearthed in archaeological finds, with pronounced breasts and bellies, highlighting the feminine aspects associated with reproduction and fertility. These figures have been found in graves where both women and men are surrounded by objects of power and authority, without gender distinctions[37].

Maritxu Guler associates this symbolism with the following qualities of the card: "Feminine progress, intelligent woman, understanding, educated, full of charms. Marks distinction, elegance, courtesy. Balance and problem-solving abilities, capacity to penetrate the soul of beings. Fertile and creative thought. Intensely loyal woman and wonderful companion" (Guler, 1976, p. 26).

____

37. For more details, see "The Chalice and the Blade" by Riane Eisler (1990), the version published by Editorial Cuatro Vientos contains an interesting introduction by Humberto Maturana about what he calls matriztic culture.

IIII The Emperor

In the GET, the fourth arcanum fo-llows the line of the Marseille decks, but like The Empress, it presents some subtle variations that are interesting. The character is a mature man with gray hair and beard, sitting on a cube with his legs crossed. He is richly dres-sed and crowned, holding an imperial scepter in his right hand. He is asso-ciated with the Sun and the correspon-ding letter in the Hebrew alphabet is ד (dalet), associated with realization.

As a natural consort of The Empress, his gaze[38] is directed to the left, right where The Empress would be if the cards were arranged in numerical or-der from left to right. Unlike the Mar-seille deck, this character does not have the imperial eagle shield and is also not adorned with a pendant necklace. Following the same line as The Empress, this character is seated on a cube associated with the number 4 and materiality, a more abstract figure than the traditional throne preferred in the Tarot of Marseille.

Another aspect in which this character differs from the Tarot of Marseille is in the crown. Unlike traditional crowns, this one

---

38. The "game of gazes" is an intriguing observation and card rea-ding tool that stems from analyzing the direction of the gaze of the card's character and relating it to the card in that location. If one wishes to delve deeper into this methodology, "El libro de oro: el Tarot de Marsella reconstruido" by Rodes and Sánchez (2014) is a recommen-ded resource. This approach provides a unique perspective in interpre-ting the tarot, as it considers the implied interactions and connections between different cards based on the direction of the characters' gazes, offering deeper insights and nuanced readings.

sprouts two deer antlers, opening an interesting perspective for the arcanum. According to the Celtic European tradition, rulers during their coronation ceremonies were empowered to represent the horned god known as Cernunnos, a god of nature and trees, as well as fertility and renewal, due to the deer's ability to renew its antlers every year. This god was also known among the Celts as the Great Father.

However, the tradition of the horned god is so ancient in Europe that it dates back to the Upper Paleolithic, meaning it is over 12,000 years old. Evidence of this can be found in the Trois Frères cave in France. Among various engravings in this cave, there is a prominent depiction of a man draped in deer skin, wearing deer antlers on his head. Anthropologist Margaret Murray describes this figure:

Illustration 10: picture Henri Breuil

"The figure is of a man wrapped in deer skin, wearing the antlers of the deer on his head. The animal's skin covers the man's entire body; hands and feet are drawn as if seen through transparent material, informing the viewer that the figure is a human being in disguise." (Murray, 2006).

This is not the only site with such imagery; other caves like Lascaux in southern France or Altamira in northern Spain contain Paleolithic cave paintings where depictions of deer and other horned animals play a prominent role.

In the literary field, Marion Zimmer Bradley (2000) presents a beautiful literary version in "The Mists of Avalon," linking King Arthur to this story. This novel retells the Arthurian saga from a feminine perspective, with Morgana, a druid priestess, as the narrator. In the relevant episode, Arthur, seeking validation from ancient traditions, undergoes the ritual of becoming the stag king and achieves consecration by mating with the priestess of Avalon, thereby renewing the vows to the old cult and allowing nature to restart its cycles.

This connection links the arcanum to the figure of King Arthur, a mythical character representing earthly authority, which is precisely where the card's character reigns. Remember that the number of this triumph is four, associated with materiality and temporality.

The figure of The Emperor is covered with a cloak, which, like The Empress, is covered with leaves[39], reinforcing the idea that the emperor governs based on the cycles of nature. The Emperor-Cernunnos is the perfect consort for The Empress-Demeter; both are ritual instruments that recreate the great cycle of the seasons.

According to Maritxu Guler, the main attributes for this arcanum are: "He is a Jovian king, with his four elements, symbol of conquest, power. The door or government, initiation, the principle of latent energy. Solar hero, dispenser of vital energy. Realization" (Guler, 1976).

The Emperor, in summary, is an arcanum that is solidly situated in the world and speaks of realization in the material world, where will has played a predominant role in achieving these ends.

Reaching this arcanum and beginning to delve into the next, we can notice that Maritxu Guler has chosen to remove the religious content linked to Christianity. The Papess of other decks has been replaced by The Consultant, and both The Empress and The Emperor have been stripped of the symbolic elements that associate their figures with the idea of the rulers of the Holy Roman Empire, such as the imperial shield.

---

39. The illustration on the card can lead to misinterpretation, and one might mistakenly think they are feathers, as pointed out by Christine Payne-Towler (Payne-Towler, 2006).

V The Master

This card, like the Papess in other decks, has been a subject of controversy throughout its history. During the period when the first decks were created, the mere inclusion of the Pope in a divinatory game was heretical to the Church, let alone a female figure in this position.

For this reason, the "heretical" name of The Pope in the Tarot of Marseille was replaced in some decks with names like The Hierophant in the Waite-Smith deck, the High Priest, or The Master in the GET. Regardless of the name, it refers to a figure whose authority stems from the spiritual realm. To illustrate this concept, remember that "hierophant" comes from the Greek (ιεροφάντης)[40] meaning 'one who reveals the sacred.'

The Pope's image in a traditional Marseille deck depicts an older, bearded man, wearing the papal tiara[41] on his head and holding the ferula[42] in his left hand. He stands between two columns, blessing two people at his feet, who could be disciples or bishops, as indicated by the hat one of them wears.

The card numbered five is titled The Master, which distances this character from the Church, but not from its symbolism. The reason why Maritxu Guler made this choice is unknown, but it's worth remembering that the presence of the Pope in the Tarot

40. "Hieros" = sacred (ιερό) and "fante" (φάντης), the one who shows.

41. This crown is the triregnum, meaning it is a triple crown. Its explanation is uncertain; one theory suggests it was made to match the emperors of the Holy Roman Empire.

42. The ferula is the staff carried by the pope, which is topped at its upper end by a cross.

has always been controversial, and the GET was created in 1976, the last year of dictator Francisco Franco's rule in Spain. During this time, the Catholic Church had a strong presence in all aspects of society, which was reinforced under Franco. Perhaps Guler, wanting to distance herself from this controversy, opted for the name given to this arcana.

Nonetheless, The Master is a fitting name for the symbolism of this arcana. A master is someone who has gathered knowledge or wisdom to exercise magisterium, who commands the spiritual aspects of any doctrine. The figure in the GET is an older man with gray hair and beard, bareheaded, standing between columns, before two disciples whom he is blessing. He does not hold a ferula, but the seven-pointed cross, usually adorning papal staffs, is inscribed on his chest. His cloak is fastened with a brooch featuring a five-pointed star.

From above, amidst clouds and sun rays, a hand emerges, making the classic priestly blessing gesture, pointing to the master, thus establishing that his authority comes from the celestial sphere.

This card is associated with the sign of Aries and the fifth letter ה (he) of the Hebrew alphabet, generally linked to inspiration.

According to Maritxu Guler in her instruction booklet, "This card represents the virtuous spiritual director, to whom one turns with faith. It indicates the resolution of marital problems. Well-being, calm, indulgence, gentleness" (Guler, 1976, p. 28).

In the symbolic analysis we have been following, we said that The Emperor reigns over the material world, as his number is four, associated with the four elements. In The Master, the associated number is five, and as it is apparent, this transcends the four material elements, corresponding to what the Greeks called quintessence, and sometimes ether. This element is so subtle that it can only be breathed by the gods, as Plato states in The Timaeus.

Thus, The Master is one who has achieved transcendence over the material world, and his natural realm is the spiritual world.

VI The Two Paths

In traditional decks, this card is named The Lover or The Lovers, but the GET opts to title the arcana, The Two Paths. However, this is where the difference ends; in other aspects, especially the essential ones, the card is consistent with the Tarot de Marseille.

The triumph of The Two Paths depicts a young man between two women at a crossroads, each attempting to draw the man to her side, as if inviting him to follow the path she is on.

Above the man and the two women, there is a winged cherub pointing an arrow at the man. This angel has its eyes uncovered. I mention this last point because in other representations the angel appears blindfolded, alluding to the idea that love is blind.

This arcana symbolizes a crucial decision in a person's life, hence the man must choose which path to take. The options presented to him are a young woman dressed in red with long hair (pleasure); and the other, a mature woman dressed in blue with generous breasts (virtue), short hair, and a tiara or headband, offering a fruit in her left hand.

The Two Paths, or The Lovers as it is named in the Marseille deck, has evolved from a historical perspective, depicting different situations alluding to marriage or matrimonial commitment, and the images chosen at each moment allude to the era in which the respective deck was crafted. However, the central theme has always maintained the idea that the arcana refers to a fundamental decision in a person's life.

This card's symbolism is ancient and can be found in the 'Pythagorean Y', obviously referring to the disjunction that this letter presents.

The central theme: Making a decision between two alternatives; was frequently presented by Greek philosophers using Hercules the demigod as an example.

This arcana presents the classic decision of Hercules, who, before starting his labors, must choose between virtue and pleasure. The card is an apt representation of this classic myth, as it shows a man accompanied by two women, one dressed for pleasure and the other for virtue.

Another possibility, which does not exclude the previous one, is considered by Maritxu Guler herself: "It is the young, strong, smiling man (from number 1) who reappears in the Tarot with number VI." (1976, p. 29). That is, it is the magician, The Consultant, who is having to decide between two women, and we can assume that those accompanying him are The Consultant and The Empress, the young woman and the mature woman, respectively.

The card presents an apparently contradictory situation raised by the following: It is the woman dressed in blue, representing virtue, who is offering the man a fruit.

If we draw an analogy from this situation to the biblical legend of the Garden of Eden, where Eve offers Adam a fruit from the forbidden tree, leading to the Fall, we encounter the paradox that it is virtue "tempting" the central character of the card.

To resolve this paradox, we need to remember that in the biblical legend, the forbidden tree is the tree of knowledge. If we distance ourselves from the moral interpretation the Church has made of this scene, it begins to make sense that virtue offers a fruit to the character, as it will provide knowledge, and if we follow the biblical text, their eyes will be opened.

Reinforcing this perspective, Jehovah, upon expelling Adam and Eve from the Garden of Eden, acknowledges that by eating the fruit of the forbidden tree, they have acquired knowledge and have thus become "like one of us". Consequently, he warns:

"Now, then, lest he put forth his hand and take also of the tree of life, and eat, and live forever" (Jerusalem Bible, 1972, pp. 3, 22).

This card is associated with the sign Taurus and with the letter ﬠ (vau) of the Hebrew alphabet, which represents trial.

From a geometric perspective, this card is associated with the hexagon, a six-sided figure, and also with a six-pointed star, known as the Star of David. This figure is generated from two interlaced triangles, speaking to the dual nature of the arcana, similar to the symbolism of arcana number II, The Consultant. In this case, the underlying attractions and oppositions are more complex than those of the second arcana in the deck.

According to Maritxu Guler's instruction booklet, referring to the central character of this card, she states: "He hesitates between Vice and Virtue. Above the group, Love extends its threatening bow and veils the Sun of truth. Letter, number, and astrological sign mark the Union and the Trial." (Guler, 1976, p. 29). That is, she echoes the tradition associated with the dilemma assigned to this arcana.

In the context of a reading, this card presents the consultant with a situation in which a decision must be made between two alternatives, which may seem forced. It is reasonable for the reader to invite the consultant to view their situation with more perspective, which often reveals solutions not apparent at first glance.

VII The Chariot of Hermes

The seventh card of the GET is named The Chariot of Hermes, usually simply titled The Chariot in the Tarot of Marseilles and other traditional decks. Maritxu Guler has chosen to attribute this chariot to Hermes, the god from Greek mythology and a figure in esotericism known as Hermes Trismegistus or "thrice-great Hermes." With this decision, the author again leads us to the legend of Persephone and Demeter, in which Hermes played a role.

Typically, this arcana features a victorious young man on a chariot pulled by two horses, and the GET has maintained this tradition. It slightly differs from the Tarot of Marseilles, as it includes a canopy covering the chariot.

The character in this card is a young man, possibly the hesitant protagonist from the previous arcana, The Two Paths, who has made a decision leading to victory. He is driving the chariot, seated almost astride, unlike the Tarot of Marseilles, where the charioteer stands under the canopy. The place where the GET character is seated has a wicker backrest.

The victorious hero is crowned and holds arrows or lightning bolts in his left hand, both symbols of his victory. In his right hand, he firmly yet gently holds the reins of the horses pulling the chariot. Here again, there is a difference from the Marseilles deck, where the charioteer has no reins, as they are not present. This subtle difference is significant, as the control the charioteer exerts over the horses is an expression of his will and doesn't require a physical medium.

This point is noteworthy because the horses typically appear to be facing the same direction, yet their bodies seem to be heading towards different goals. The subtle mastery of the charioteer, this ability to unite different wills, is a condition often distinguishing mastery. Therefore, the way the charioteer exerts this influence on others is not irrelevant. If this ability in the Tarot of Marseilles is exercised subtly, immaterially, without physical reins to direct different aspects of the will towards a goal, it differs from the way the GET charioteer exercises this influence, relying on material reins.

The shape of the chariot is cubic, following the traditional form found in most Marseilles decks. The character, in turn, forms a triangular figure, with legs apart and a wide base, up to the crown. Combining these two elements from a geometric perspective, we get a triangle on a square, a three-sided figure on a four-sided figure. Equivalently, we can consider the number seven constituted by a three-sided figure plus (+) a four-sided figure.

Both figures that constitute the number seven speak of stability. On the one hand, the square is associated with the four elements and the material world; on the other, the triangle, a figure of great balance when well-proportioned. By combining them, forming a triangle over a square, this idea of stability is reinforced. In other words, the hero featured in this card can maintain this situation as long as he keeps the balance that originated it.

This card is associated with the zodiac sign Gemini and the Hebrew letter zayin (ז), linked to victory.

Maritxu herself points out the victory aspect of the arcana but also recognizes that "to achieve victory, one must have balanced physical and moral forces. Knowledge of adversities and preparation to overcome them" (Guler, 1976, p. 30). She adds that the person in this situation rides "...at the height of success and popularity." Lastly, she highlights an aspect often overlooked in those who achieve success but is vitally important for its sustainability: "Tact in governing" (1976, p. 30).

As previously mentioned, Maritxu Guler likely wanted to relate this arcana to the Persephone-Demeter relationship from the arcanas The Consultant and The Empress by naming it The Chariot of Hermes.

In the Greek mythological legend referenced in the previous arcana, after Hades abducted Persephone and took her to the underworld, her mother, Demeter, in her grief, disrupted the cycle of nature's renewal, leading to a state of desolation on Earth.

This situation became unbearable, and Zeus, after initially avoiding Demeter, agreed that Persephone should be returned to her mother, accepting Hades' condition that she not consume food until her rescue, as anyone who tasted the food of the dead could not return to life. Zeus commissioned Hermes to bring Persephone back from the underworld.

Hermes embarked on his downward journey in his chariot. During the wait, Persephone ate some pomegranate seeds. Cunningly, Hades remained silent until Hermes arrived.

When Hermes was about to return, Ascalaphus, the gardener of Hades, testified that he saw Persephone eat pomegranate seeds. Hades sent Ascalaphus along with Persephone and Hermes back to testify before Zeus. Knowing this, the king of gods finally resolves in a Solomonic way that Persephone should return to Hades with her husband for part of the year and spend the other part with her mother on Earth. These back and forth journeys of the Earth's daughter to and from Hades gave rise to the cycle of the seasons and the perpetual renewal of nature.

It is the charioteer's ability to reconcile divergent forces that has led him to achieve success.

Second septenary

The second septenary begins with Justice and closes with Temperance, that is, it starts and ends with a virtue. In this second cycle, The Elder (The Hermit in Marseille Tarot), The Wheel of Fortune, Strength, The Pillory (The Hanged Man in Marseille Tarot), and the number XIII arcana accompany the two aforementioned arcana.

In general terms, the first septenary explored themes within the realm of the human and the earthly. In contrast, the second septenary presents The Fool with more abstract and universal themes, such as the virtues expressed in Justice, Strength, Temperance, and possibly prudence in The Elder. If one doesn't want to interpret this virtue in The Elder, it would still represent wisdom. Alongside the universality of the virtues, there are motifs that also possess a certain universality, such as fortune in The Wheel of Fortune, generous detachment towards others in The Pillory, and finally, the most shared theme among all living beings, which is death, reflected in the number XIII arcana.

If we consider Illustration 1, where the Major Arcana are arranged in septenaries, we can see in the seventh column, on the right, the image of The Chariot of Hermes, in the first row. This triumph concludes the first septenary and its meaning is an indicator of success, accomplishment, showing that The Fool's first journey has ended victoriously after facing the decision posed by The Two Paths.

Similarly, the second septenary concludes with Temperance, an arcana that signifies balance, after facing the most demanding test of all, death in the number XIII arcana. The temperance acquired in the challenges of this cycle prepares the traveler for even more transcendent trials, which will be seen in the third septenary.

Following the arrangement of septenaries in Illustration 1, we can see that in the third row, above Temperance, is The World, concluding its respective cycle. That is to say, the final card of each septenary is its synthesis and conclusion.

In the second septenary, Temperance indicates that the intermediate cycle of personal development has been completed, gaining self-mastery: the condition of mastery and readiness to project oneself into the future, facing the demands of the next stage of one's journey.

The first septenary placed the traveler in learning situations that were within the realm of the human and the earthly. In contrast, the second septenary will challenge those who have embarked on this journey of self-discovery to integrate more abstract and universal challenges, such as the virtues expressed in the cards I have mentioned: Justice, Strength, Temperance, and prudence in The Elder.

You will also have to overcome challenges such as that of The Wheel of Fortune, where the challenge is to learn from the triviality of the material world, the caprices of circumstantial success, upon which, more transcendent aspects of life are built.

In The Pillory (The Hanged Man in the Marseille deck), the instrument of torture is voluntarily accepted, since the renunciation of oneself for the good of others is the way to overcome egotistic behavior and begin to establish relationships based on love with others.

Finally, you must face the most decisive test of all, one's own death in the thirteenth arcane. This challenge, the most transcendent in a person's life, prepares us to be reborn into a new life. If we accept dying to what we are, we can acquire temperance, which opens the path of the spiritual world, available in the third septenary.

VIII The Justice

Regarding the Solomonic judgment made by Zeus in the case of Persephone and Hades, the god of the underworld, Maritxu introduces this concept in the eighth arcana of the deck, The Justice.

The traditional representation of this card in the Marseille decks shows the image of justice as the Romans used to depict in the goddess Iustitia: a blind-folded woman holding a scale in one hand and a sword in the other.

In the Tarot of Marseille, this figure appears seated in a wide chair, with un-covered eyes and crowned. She wields a bare sword in her right hand, with the hilt resting on her leg and pointing upwards. The scale is held in her left hand and is slightly unba-lanced, to indicate that what is just is not necessarily equal.

Generally, the scale is associated with a meaning of impartiality, hence, in some periods, justice was depicted blindfolded, so it could not be influenced by situations external to the merits of the case. Regarding the sword, it has two symbolic scopes. One is rectitude, due to its shape, and the other is power, which is necessary to enforce the decisions of justice.

This figure presents some modifications in the GET that are not significant and that enhance the general meaning of the card.

The character that appears is an older man, with white beards, who is also seated and with uncovered sight, wearing a crown on his head. The figure evokes at first glance a royal character. His attire is complemented by a white tunic, girded with a belt, and a blue cloak.

The sword is in his left hand, as in his right he holds a child, an infant. He is wielding the sword in a gesture oriented to cut the baby.

The entire assembly of the arcane brings to mind the image of King Solomon in the act of dividing a child in the famous Solomonic judgment.

The story is based on the account of King Solomon narrated in the First Book of Kings (Jerusalem Bible, 1972, p. 3: 16-28), where the situation of two women who come to Solomon to resolve a dispute they have over a newborn is recounted.

One of the women tells the king that she fell asleep shortly after breastfeeding her son and that when she woke up in the morning to feed him, she found him dead beside her. The mother claims that the dead baby is the other woman's and that she, during the night while she slept, stealthily exchanged the children without waking her.

The second woman maintains that the living child is her son and that the dead little one is the son of the first woman.

After hearing the pleas of both women, King Solomon addressed his men, ordering them to bring a sword and to divide the child in two, giving half to each woman. Upon hearing this, the true mother spoke to the king, asking him to give the child to the other woman but not to harm him. Meanwhile, the other woman said: "Neither yours nor mine. Cut him!"

Upon hearing the women, the king made a decision and ordered that the child be given to the woman who was willing to give up her son, stating that she was his mother.

This simple story is rich in symbolism, not only of a legal order but also profoundly revealing of human nature. Delving into all the details involved in it is beyond the scope of this work. However, it is worth mentioning aspects like truth associated with renunciation.

The gesture of the true mother, who prefers to give up her son, allows her to recover him, and this tells us that sometimes, to move forward, it is necessary or more convenient to yield, rather than to maintain an intransigent position.

On the other hand, the act, seemingly cruel at first, along with the attitude of renunciation assumed by the mother, allows the truth to come to light and reveals who is indeed the mother, with which the truth can emerge.

This last point is what, in my opinion, most clearly symbolizes the concept of justice that the arcane wants to convey. Therefore, the story evoked by the figure is a very appropriate replacement for the unbalanced scale carried by the character of this arcana in traditional decks.

The success that Maritxu Guler achieves with this way of expressing symbolism is that it easily conveys to the consultant the meaning of The Justice through the story of King Solomon, as it is generally known by all people educated within the Judeo-Christian and Muslim traditions, whether they practice these religions or not.

On the other hand, the representation of the scale to convey this symbolism is more abstract and most of the time it is more difficult to communicate through this medium.

The meaning that Maritxu Guler assigns to this card in her instruction booklet, speaks of a: "Complete person, thoughtful, capable of understanding and solving different problems leaving everyone satisfied. Well-justified actions. Good administrator. Lawsuit won" (1976, p. 31).

This card is associated with the Cancer sign and the letter ח (heth) of the Hebrew alphabet, related to balance.

Another important aspect of this arcane is that it is associated with one of the four cardinal virtues: justice. The other two virtues represented in current decks are strength and temperance, in the cards of the same name. The virtue absent in contemporary decks is prudence.

The virtues I have mentioned are qualities of the human being, coined in classical antiquity and canonized by Plato in "The Republic," where he added prudence to justice, fortitude, and temperance. Since then, they have been a part of philosophical and religious reflection on ethical and moral issues.

Subsequently, Christianity added to the four cardinal virtues three theological virtues: faith, hope, and charity. The religious argument for considering these virtues is that they are habits that God incorporates into the human being to direct their intelligence and will towards God Himself.

Some classic decks, such as the Visconti-Sforza Tarot, even though it included only one of the cardinal virtues: strength, included the three theological virtues: faith, hope, and charity. Other decks also included some or all of the theological virtues, but this custom fell into disuse, especially once the Tarot of Marseille standardized the card decks.

VIII The Hermit

The card in the ninth position has a variation in its name compared to traditional decks, such as the Tarot of Marseille, where it is known as The Hermit (L' Hermite). However, the GET presents a triumph with the name The Old Man. Despite this difference in name, there are no major differences in its graphic representation, maintaining the themes that have become standard in this card, with some minor variations.

The Hermit of the Marseille deck depicts an old, bearded man, dressed in what could be a habit, holding a lantern in his right hand and a staff in his left.

The Old Man in the GET maintains an important part of this representation. He is an elderly, mostly bald man with white hair and beard. He wears what appears to be a dark blue habit and over it, a green cloak.

In his right hand, he carries a lantern with a candle as its light source, and in his left, the characteristic staff carried by the character in other decks.

His environment is a place removed from civilization, surrounded by nature. Beside the old man is a male deer with the distinctive antlers of this type of animal, surely to show his connection with nature[43].

The figure evokes someone who has retired from the "mundane noise" to have a peaceful dwelling, where he can dedicate

---

43. Se podría pensar en Cerunnos, el dios astado de los celtas, vínculo que examino con más detalle en los arcanos IIII El Emperador y en el XV, Aker.

himself to reflection and meditation, away from the hustle and bustle and disturbances of city life.

The figure embodies the idea that the character has dedicated himself to a search, where the central focus is internal search. For this reason, he wishes to avoid the distractions that interactions with others imply. This symbolism speaks of solitude as the best and only possible companion when embarking on this path.

In interpretation, the arcane suggests to the consultant to distance themselves from others to carry out the necessary reflection that will allow finding the light to illuminate the path of the answers they are seeking for their situation.

Among the variations in the iconographic representation that this arcane has experienced, there are some aspects to consider to understand its definitive representation. In the earliest decks, this card represented time, a symbolic character typical of the late Middle Ages, who carried an hourglass instead of the lamp he now holds in his hand.

The arcane evolved from this character to the image it has today, presenting a series of questions about its origin and symbolism. Some see in the card a monk from the Capuchin order (Méndez Filesi, 2016c), which derived from the Franciscans, others consider that the old man would be the Greek philosopher Diogenes the Cynic, and the third hypothesis is that it would represent the missing cardinal virtue: prudence.

The propositions that seem most interesting to me from a symbolic point of view are the last two, so I will focus my attention on them.

The possibility that it represents Diogenes is well-founded, as the philosopher, native of Sinope, settled in Athens where he lived as a vagabond, dwelling in a barrel. He made extreme poverty a virtue and roamed the city streets with a lit lamp during the day, searching for men.

According to his teachings, human beings should live self-sufficiently, naturally, and without the luxuries of society, since honors and riches are false achievements, and wisdom consists in freeing oneself from desires and minimizing needs.

The philosophical tenets of Diogenes coincide with the symbolism of the card, and although the creators of this image might not have had the Greek philosopher in mind, it perfectly fits the concept they wish to convey.

The other possibility is that it represents prudence, one of the four cardinal virtues, since the other three are present in this deck, in the Marseille deck, and in most traditional decks.

In defense of this hypothesis, it must be considered that, just as justice is the foundational virtue on which the others are based, prudence is the principal virtue, as it governs the soul due to its knowledge of what is good. One aspect that characterizes The Old Man is wisdom, either because he possesses it due to his years or because the character's attitude indicates he is in its pursuit. This characteristic of the arcane proposed by the GET makes it a good candidate to represent the virtue of prudence.

On the other hand, if we consider the three cardinal virtues that are included in the deck: Justice number VIII, Strength number XI, and Temperance number XIIII; we see that all of them are in the second septenary, so the inclusion of prudence in this same septenary has a certain logic.

As I mentioned when discussing the properties of the septenaries in the respective section, the first septenary refers to human properties and characters, the second to abstract qualities, and the third to transcendent or celestial aspects. Therefore, the inclusion of a virtue like prudence in this second septenary is consistent with the proposed organizational principle for the major arcana.

The association of this card is with the Leo sign and the ט letter (teth) of the Hebrew alphabet linked to prudence.

The meaning that Martixu Guler assigns to it in her instruction booklet is: "See and be silent. Prudence even in the smallest things. If speech is silver, silence is golden. Refrain from commenting. Avoid politics. Vigilance, discretion, caution. It also marks concentration and deep meditation" (1976, p. 32).

X The Wheel of Fortune

The Wheel of Fortune in the Marseille decks depicts a wheel with three strange characters: one climbing, another descending, and the third, at the top of the wheel, crowned and holding a sword in his left hand. The dynamism of the figure invites us to reflect on the ups and downs of life and the circumstantial nature of what we consider good or bad fortune at any given moment. The character at the top should have clarity about these changing situations.

The GET has chosen an unorthodox approach for this card and introduces some modifications in its representation.

The animals used are atypical for traditional decks. On a tree branch sits a crowned monkey holding a wind-whirled pinwheel. Below the tree is a large white bear pushing a stone wheel with its left hand and supporting itself with the other hand on the tree.

On the tree, in a filigree that stretches across the card, is the figure of Janus, the Roman two-faced god. According to tradition, this god looks to the east and west simultaneously, to the past and also to the future, and in this sense, he has the same symbolism as the sphinx that appears in decks such as Oswald Wirth's or Waite-Smith's, which is capable of contemplating beyond the moments and circumstances of the present. This distant horizon view is the advice of this arcane for those who are saddened by circumstantial misfortune or exultant with momentary success.

The two animals, although atypical, complement the overall symbolism of the card. The monkey on the tree, in a beneficial position, is accompanied by the pinwheel that spins according to the whims of the wind. This animal has precedents in the Eteilla deck, a great promoter of tarot in 18th-century France, who used a similar figure to illustrate this card in his deck (Payne-Towler, 2006, p. 20).

The bear under the tree bears the burdensome load of the wheel to indicate that it is in a disadvantaged situation and must carry the load, just as it happens to someone in a situation of misfortune.

In the early Renaissance, it was common to illustrate fortune with a wheel, onto which those aspiring to success would climb, as can be seen in a 15th-century French version of Boccaccio's book, "De casibus", which deals with famous successful people in history who inevitably fall.

The presence of Janus in this arcane refers to the idea of duality that is very strong in the card. According to the Roman pantheon, Janus was associated with the concept of transition, as his image was placed at the entrances of homes, representing the transition from the outside of the house to a protected place inside the home.

By extension of this concept, the god Janus came to represent the transition of the seasons, as one of his faces represents the summer solstice and the other the winter solstice, signifying the perpetual change from one season to another and vice versa.

The ability of the god Janus to look in two directions simultaneously: east and west, past and future, allows those who heed the advice of the card to balance the situations they are going through at the time of the consultation.

The general meaning of the card speaks of changing situations, which should be taken advantage of when luck smiles, to be patient when fortune is adverse, and to have the wisdom to understand that these two moments are just that, in the eternal cycle of renewal that is fate.

As a warning, the card, drawing on popular wisdom, advises that the higher a person rises, the harder their fall will be and that the more desolate one feels in misfortune, the more they will enjoy coming out of that situation.

The meaning that Guler assigns to it in her instruction booklet is: "Fortune, happy initiative. Zenith. Do not let good opportunities slip away, gain in gambling, lottery, roulette, etc. Well-paid work. Progress. Well-functioning enterprises. Advance. Good health" (1976, p. 33).

The association of this card is with the Virgo sign and the letter ' (yod) of the Hebrew alphabet associated with fortune.

From a numerological perspective, this card closes the first ten arcana and by reduction (1 + 0 = 1) it leads back to the first arcane, that is, a restart, a return to the beginning, which reinforces the circular concept found in the central idea of its symbolism. No matter what situations are faced, they are changeable, and what is considered misfortune today, will inevitably change tomorrow.

XI Strength

In this arcane, Maritxu Guler makes small variations, which, while respecting the traditional symbolism, add interest to the card.

In the Marseille deck, the arcane is titled La Force (Strength) in its Spanish translation and depicts a woman opening the jaws of a lion. She wears a hat on her head that suggests the representation of the infinity symbol (∞).

The corresponding arcane in the GET is named La Fortaleza (Strength), one of the four cardinal virtues. However, the image presented is not the usual one in the iconography of the time for this cardinal virtue.

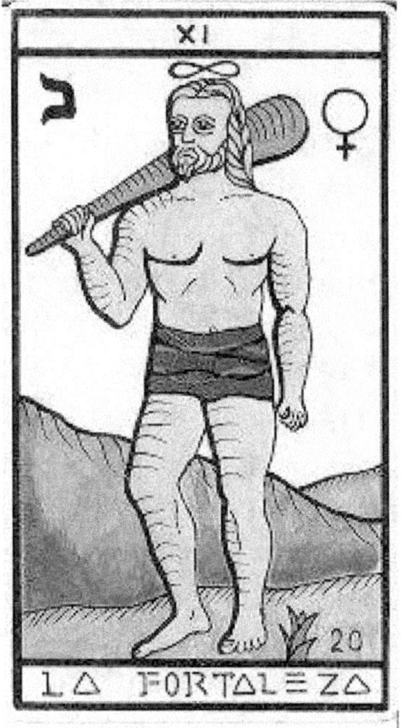

The character depicted in the card is a young or middle-aged man with long hair and a beard. He is almost naked, with only a tight-fitting trunks covering him. In his right hand, he holds a club resting on his shoulder. Over his head, the infinity symbol is explicitly drawn.

From the perspective of the historical evolution of the decks, this card has been a subject of controversy, given the doubt about which character it alludes to, and the clearest options have leaned towards Hercules or Samson, since in traditional decks, a lion accompanies the main character, and both heroes have stories in which this animal plays a prominent role: Hercules in the mission of the Nemean lion and Samson on a journey to see Delilah.

Hercules' story is the first of the twelve labors this hero undertakes (Graves, 1993). According to the story, the lion was a huge beast that ravaged the surroundings of the city of Nemea. The beast had a particular characteristic; its skin was impervious to iron, bronze, or stone, making it very difficult to kill.

Eurystheus, king of Argolis, tasked Hercules with killing and skinning the lion. After a prolonged search, as no one could give him clues about the animal, he found it and attacked, first with arrows, then with his sword, and finally with his club. On none of these occasions did he manage to harm the beast with his blows. So, he finally decided to fight the beast hand-to-hand. In the fray, Hercules managed to wrap his arm around the lion's head and thus killed it by asphyxiation.

The most important moral of the story, and which is relevant to the arcane, is that strength alone, we might say brute force, was not enough to defeat the beast, and it was necessary for Hercules to apply his strength with intelligence to achieve success.

This lesson is very consistent with the dual nature of the symbolism of the card. Applying numerological reduction to the number 11 of the card, we obtain 2 as a result of adding 1 + 1, the digits that compose The Strength. As seen in the second arcane, The High Priestess, which is a card of dual nature, it expresses complementary forces, attraction or rejection. This is precisely what the eleventh arcane conveys, especially in the Marseille decks, where a woman overcomes the lion, because it is strength applied with gentleness or intelligence that achieves success. In the GET, this symbolic aspect is considered, as the Venus sign associated with the feminine is drawn.

This reaffirms that the most appropriate name for this arcane is Strength and not Force, as the latter speaks of a single energy directed linearly to achieve a purpose, while Strength considers the dual aspect of force combined with intelligence.

In the case of Samson, the story is narrated in The Bible (1972, Judges 14), where it is said that Samson asked his parents to find him a wife among the Philistine women. On his way to the place where the young woman lived, a lion appeared, and the hero killed it with his hands.

On the return trip with his fiancée, he saw that in the lion's carcass there was a beehive, so he scraped off the honey and ate it. During the wedding, he proposed a riddle to the attendees: "Out of the eater, something to eat; out of the strong, something sweet" (1972, Judges 14). After a series of pressures on Samson's wife, they manage to obtain the answer, so the guests reply to the hero: "What is sweeter than honey, and what is stronger than a lion?" (1972, Judges 14).

This last part of the plot expresses the symbolism of the Strength arcane, as the honey inside the lion combines strength and sweetness. Considering that a very specific detail is used to represent a more universal symbolism, which is what an arcane requires, we can examine the entirety of Samson's story. His strength lies in something as soft and delicate as hair, and his story ends with a Machiavellian act of intelligence, where after patiently waiting for his hair to grow back while blind, he asks to be placed next to the columns supporting the temple and brings them down with his regained strength.

Virtues are traditionally represented with a feminine gender, and tarot decks have followed this tradition. Hence, it is noteworthy that the GET has altered this custom. However, in the historical evolution of tarot decks, strength has been personified by a male character in decks as old as the Piermont-Morgan Bergamo deck[44] from 1451. In this representation, it takes the form of a man wielding a club against a lion lying at his feet. The figure mentioned bears a striking resemblance to that presented by Maritxu Guler.

The association with Samson can also be seen from the historical perspective of the graphic evolution of card decks. For instance, the Medici tarot from the 15th century illustrates this card with a female character knocking down a column, clearly alluding to the biblical scene where Samson destroys the temple of Dagon by bringing down its columns (Judges 16, 1972).

The meaning assigned by Guler in her instruction booklet is: "Strength, courage, resolution. Moral energy. One must move forward with faith, as obstacles are mere phantoms. Intelligence dominating brutality. Virility. Spiritual potency. Conquest, courage. Virtue" (1976, p. 34).

The association of this card is with the planet Venus and the letter כ (kaf) of the Hebrew alphabet, related to strength. This as-

---

44. This deck is also known by the name of Francesco Sforza.

sociation aligns with the broader themes of vitality, virility, and overcoming challenges through a combination of physical strength and moral fortitude, as embodied in the character of Samson and the traditional representations of strength in tarot iconography.

XII The Gibbet

This is one of the arcana where Mari-txu Guler deviates from the orthodoxy represented by the Tarot of Marseille, starting with the name. In the Marseille decks, it is titled The Hanged Man in English[45], and it depicts a character hanging upside down, suspended by the left foot from a horizontal cross-beam. The crossbeam is hung between two vertical posts, each with six sawed-off branches.

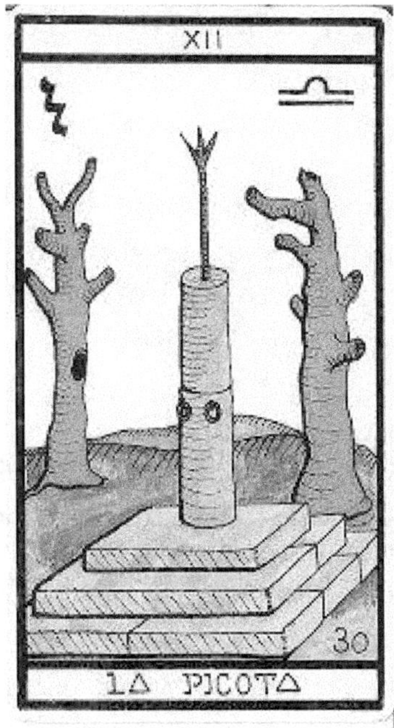

The man appears in an attitude of slight unconcern as if the punishment does not affect him. His free leg forms a cross or a triangle over the other. His hands are behind his back. In some decks, like the Oswald Wirth, coins fall from the character.

In this arcane, the GET proposes a very different image, and at first, it is hard to find the relationship with the symbolism of the card. To start, it lacks a human figure, and in the central position, there is an instrument of torture known as a pike or gibbet. It has a pointed object at its top, ending in three spikes. On the front side, there are two rings, and it is placed on a platform with three levels or steps.

On either side of this figure are the two vertical posts with six cut-off branches on each.

To understand the symbolism of this arcane, I started from the Tarot of Marseille, as it seemed clearer to me. The figure of the hanged man reminded me of the stories or legends about Peter and Andrew, the apostles. According to these stories, when Peter

---

45. Le Pendu in French comes from pendre = to hang, so in this language it can mean the hanged or the hanged man indifferently.

was captured and prepared for his crucifixion, he asked to be placed upside down, as he considered himself unworthy to die like Jesus Christ. Perhaps for this reason, an inverted cross appears on the back of the papal chair.

Regardless of the veracity of the story of Peter's death, an inverted cross or a character hanged upside down is considered a symbol of humility. This meaning begins to bring us closer to the deep concept of this arcane. As the character seems to be voluntarily undergoing this punishment and is also bearing it with composure, it implies an act of renunciation, which is also carried out with humility.

In the Medici Tarot, the representation of this arcane is much more direct and shows Christ transfigured before the disciples. Only the atmosphere of independence from the power of the Church in Medici Florence allowed the explicit depiction of Jesus Christ on this card. But surely in other parts of Europe, it was not possible, and that is why this up-side-down hanging character was preferred, in which the crucifixion of the savior of Christians is evoked elusively through the Apostle Peter. In this fact, there is an act of great generosity, as Christ, having the power to avoid it, accepts to die on the cross to save the sins of the world.

In my opinion, here lies the key to the symbolism of the arcane, suggesting to a consultant that to address their current situation, they must renounce part of their ego and sacrifice for others if they wish to resolve it. This generous act allows them to transcend, which is very important in this arcane, especially considering that the next card is Death.

Having made the above reflection, we are in a position to understand the image proposed by Maritxu Guler. The gibbet was a medieval torture instrument where prisoners were exposed in that era, and it was common for towns in the Iberian Peninsula to have one of these instruments. I believe the author of the deck mixes this instrument with the spike, used for executions by impalement, a penalty used by the Spanish in the Middle Ages and in the Conquest of America. This is evidenced by Alonso de Ercilla y Zúñiga in his epic poem "La Araucana," which recounts the death of the toqui Caupolicán[46], who was executed by this atrocious torment.

Interestingly, this hero of resistance against the Spanish chose to sit on the spike himself, scorning his captors and without his face showing any sign of the terrible pain he was experiencing, which coincidentally makes him consistent with the meaning of the arcane. However, I consider this fact a mere coincidence, as the figure of Caupolicán does not belong to the European cultural imagination, and I have no evidence to suppose that the author of the deck knew of the hero through "La Araucana" or another means and decided to use his figure symbolically. Rather, everything indicates by the selected image, the gibbet, that the content of its symbolism remains within the European context.

Another novel aspect in this arcane is that the symbolism used once again eludes Christian imagery.

The meaning that Martixu Guler assigns to it in her instruction booklet is: "Idealism, self-forgetfulness. Commitment to a cause, personal sacrifice. Patriotism, apostolate. Searching for a solution to a problem. Rebirth, regeneration" (1976, p. 35).

The association of this card is with the Libra sign and the letter ל (lamed) of the Hebrew alphabet associated with violent death. The number of this letter is 30, which is printed on the card.

---

46. In Mapudungun, Kallfülikan means blue stone.

XIII Immortality

Maritxu Guler titles this arcane only in the instruction booklet, as is customary in all decks, the thirteenth arcane is unnamed, although it is popularly called "Death."

This card follows the traditional symbolism of a skeleton wielding a scythe in its right hand. The character's only clothing is a black cloak on the outside and red on the inside, adorned with symbols of the moon and stars.

The skeleton rides a huge dog, almost the size of a small horse. The animal has its jaws open, and a spiked collar surrounds its neck, with a chain allowing the skeleton to control its mount.

On the ground are strewn crowns of kings and popes, a bishop's staff, a sword, a sickle, and a head without a body. These elements represent the main figures of authority and social classes of the time. Kings, nobles, religious authorities, soldiers, and peasants are at the feet of death, which has the power to seal their fate.

In the background of the image, a temple is visible, featuring an Aten cross at its entrance. We will see this building again in the card The Cycle. The elements on the ground represent the insignificance of everyday life matters, and the temple, in the distance on the horizon, represents the transcendental, that which is beyond worldly concerns.

The origin of this arcane is related to the plague that decimated Europe at the end of the Middle Ages, particularly brutal in northern Italy in Venice, Florence, and Milan, cities from which the first known decks originate. These cities, due to their significant integration into Mediterranean trade, especially in the case of Florence and Venice, experienced particularly high and recurrent impacts of the plague, attacking these cities in successive waves.

A pandemic of this magnitude, which is estimated to have devastated between 30 to 50% of the European population, undoubtedly left an indelible mark on the collective imagination of the continent, which is expressed in the tarot with the pictorial force present in the thirteenth arcane.

Very likely, the iconographic antecedent presented by the image of this card is found in the Four Horsemen of the Apocalypse, a text attributed to the Apostle John.

> "I looked, and there before me was a pale horse! Its rider was named Death, and Hades was following close behind him. They were given power over a fourth of the earth to kill by sword, famine, and plague, and by the wild beasts of the earth." Revelation (6:8)

This image was deeply rooted in the collective thought of the creators of the tarot and is possibly one of the sources that contributed to its creation.

This arcane marks a turning point in the realm in which the cards present their motifs. Up to this point, the cards have unfolded in the world of the terrestrial, like The Emperor or The Pope, and from this arcane onwards, the motifs are of a celestial order, like The Star, The Sun, or The World. In this sense, for those who overcome death, the earthly is left behind, and a new experiential dimension opens up, where immaterial and transcendent issues become more important (Méndez Filesi, 2016b).

This allegory of death and rebirth into a new life proposed by the tarot coincides with that of religions or esoteric societies that organize their learning in symbolic and numerical keys.

Despite the intimidating appearance of the arcane, its general meaning is related to change and its inevitability, and although it may seem contradictory, the card by itself has a positive interpretation. For renewal to exist, something must be left behind. To become better people, something must change or die in the sense of "ceasing to be," to transform into new and more evolved individuals.

Negative interpretations can be given when it is accompanied by other cards that go against this change.

The meaning assigned by Martixu Guler in her instruction booklet is:

> "To the left the symbol that says: trust in the resurrection. Number and letter also mark physical and moral destruction and speak of a sure rebirth."

"Divinatory meaning. Death. Elevate your spirit and leave material things behind. Your ambitions will be cut like the grass of the meadows. (1976, p. 36)"

The association of this card is with the letter מ (mem) of the Hebrew alphabet, associated with the transformation of man. Although not graphically represented on the card, it is associated with Neptune as a zodiacal planet according to the Gra[47] correspondence pattern.

---

47. The Gra scheme of astro-alpha-numeric correspondences is named after Elijah Ben Solomon (his acronym in Hebrew is HaGra, "Ha-Gaon Rabbenu Elijah") and corresponds to an arrangement of the Tree of Life according to the oldest version of Kabbalistic doctrine. This version contrasts with that of Isaac Luria's ARI, which includes the sefirah Da'at in the scheme of the sefirot. For more details, see "God's Ambiance: Is Revealed in the Matrix of Wisdom" (Meegan, 2016, p. 31).

XIV Temperance

This arcane is one of those that has experienced the least variation since its iconography was established in canonical decks like the Tarot of Marseille. It is represented by a winged woman holding a pitcher in each of her hands, pouring liquid from one pitcher to the other.

The GET illustrates Temperance, following the established canons. In the card, a blonde woman[48] dressed in red and blue is depicted; her blouse is red, and her long skirt is blue. On her forehead, in the center, is adorned with an object that is not clearly distinguishable; it could be a brooch or a flower, as in the Tarot of Marseille.

The object itself is not important; what is relevant is that it marks the center of the forehead. In her left hand, she holds a white pitcher, and in her right, a yellow one. A liquid flows between both pitchers, and it is not clear whether the liquid is flowing upwards or downwards.

In my opinion, this ambiguity in the illustration is one of the central elements in the meaning of the arcane, as it speaks more of mixing than of simply pouring liquid from one vessel into another, where the direction can be downwards but also upwards. This will depend on the circumstance and what is required.

The consensus on the card clearly reflects what is intended to be conveyed: the character is sober and moderate, of a spiritual or angelical nature, and is mixing and distilling the subtle ener-

---

48. As are all the young or middle-aged characters, except for The Empress, who, although her hair cannot be seen, it is reasonable to assume that it is black.

gies resulting from her work, which will enable her to tackle the tasks at hand.

It is important to remember that this card follows the thirteenth arcane, so it has overcome the trial of death, and this experience provides the tranquility to face all situations with balance and measure, that is, with Temperance.

It is the last card of the second septenary, summarizing the achievement obtained in this second stage. If we consider Illustration 1 on page 29, where the major arcana are arranged in septenaries, we can see that in the seventh column, to the right of the image, The Chariot of Hermes is in the first row of this column, Temperance in the second row, and above it, in the third row, The World. As mentioned earlier, these three cards are associated because each one corresponds to the last of its respective septenary and therefore is its synthesis and conclusion.

In the case of Temperance, it is situated between The Chariot of Hermes and The World, having completed the intermediate cycle of personal development, acquiring mastery over oneself, and is in a position to project into the future, meeting the demands of the next stage of its evolution.

As we have seen, the first septenary posed challenges that were in the realm of the human, the earthly. In contrast, the second septenary has proposed to The Fool in his journey to incorporate more abstract and immaterial matters such as virtues, expressed in: Justice, Strength, Temperance, and perhaps prudence in The Hermit.

He also had to overcome trials like that of The Wheel of Fortune, where he had to learn the insignificance of the material world, or The Hanged Man, where self-renunciation for the good of others was the only way to surpass this stage. And finally, the most definitive trial of all, death itself in the thirteenth arcane, the most transcendental in a person's life, whose understanding enables us to be reborn into a new life.

From a thematic perspective, this arcane is one of the four cardinal virtues, as established by Plato, and one of the three included in a traditional tarot, along with strength and justice. This followed an evolution in line with how medieval and Renaissance philosophy considered the cardinal and theological virtues.

If we consider an oracular perspective, the card suggests to the consultant to approach the situations they are experiencing with balance and measure. To have the necessary patience to know when and how to undertake an action granted by **self-mastery.**

The meaning assigned by Guler in her instruction booklet is: "Temperance, moderation. Assess your moral and physical strengths and do not back down from obstacles; but use them little by little. Drink in moderation. Tolerant character, flexibility to adapt to circumstances" (1976, p. 37).

The association of this card is with the Scorpio sign and the letter נ (nun) of the Hebrew alphabet associated with human initiative.

Third Septenary

The third and final septenary begins with a card named Aker in this deck and concludes with The World. The other five cards of this stage of The Fool's journey, accompanying these two, are: The Tower, The Star, The Moon, The Sun, and The Cycle.

The second septenary ends with overcoming death, which allows achieving the balance of temperance. This significant step implies leaving behind the previous existence to open up to a new life that involves transcendence as its fundamental reason. Therefore, the challenges and motifs in the arcana of this stage correspond to matters beyond the earthly and even beyond universal issues like the virtues of the second septenary. This time, The Fool will tackle situations that are of a celestial, transcendent order.

This septenary is not without its trials, which begin with the first card of this cycle, Aker, as seen in Illustration 1 and continue with The Tower. In both figures, Maritxu Guler introduces symbolism from Basque traditions. In the first, aker, the Basque male goat, replaces The Devil from other decks.

Aker is also associated with the judgments of the Inquisition in Zurragamurdi, and the image chosen by the author is almost identical to one used by Eliphas Levi in "Dogma and Ritual of High Magic", with the difference that the French esotericist used the expressions "solve" and "coagula" inscribed on the arms of the character. In a figure as sexually charged as this one, this symbolism reminds us that the same energy that leads to transcendence can also lead to perdition.

The trials in this stage continue in The Tower. This arcane easily evokes the biblical story of the Tower of Babel, where humans, after the Great Flood, propose to build a tower so high it reaches the heavens. The challenge present in this story is pride and, more generally, the limitations our own ego imposes on us.

Having overcome the obstacles we set for ourselves through

the ego, it's time for The Star. This card introduces us to the celestial triad along with The Sun and The Moon. The Star recalls the story of the Star of Bethlehem, which guided three wise men from the heavens to the birth of Jesus. It brings good tidings and announces that the mission is nearing completion.

The journey continues with The Moon, an arcane that expresses emotional aspects, where melancholy and introspection predominate. It invites us to encounter and recognize our deepest moods and tendencies, those that lie in our shadow side.

After the shadows, The Sun shines with all its light. Possibly, it is the card that radiates the most energy in the entire deck, under which every project prospers. This arcane expresses that the work is reaching its culmination.

In the penultimate card of the septenary, Maritxu Guler makes a distinct choice and replaces the traditional Judgment with The Cycle, which shows two suns on a trajectory of change. Each of these celestial bodies is associated with the signs Pisces and Aquarius, respectively, to remind us of the interpretation popularized by the New Age movement about us being in a time of epochal change.

The transition announced in the previous arcane manifests in The World. The project of The Magician, now realized. The four elements are represented in the four evangelists surrounding the figure of a character who has completed themselves and, therefore, can now transcend. This depiction symbolizes the culmination of a journey, not just in terms of personal growth and development but also in the broader sense of moving into a new era or phase of existence. The World card, as the final step in The Fool's journey, signifies completion, fulfillment, and the realization of potential, indicating a state of wholeness and balanced mastery.

XV Aker

This card was the one that impressed me the most when I began to explore the GET. Its enigmatic and sexually charged character, coupled with its name, which at the time represented a great mystery to me, had a profound impact.

In the 1980s, one of the few books I could access on the subject was Eliphas Levi's "Dogma and Ritual of High Magic." The second part of this text begins with a black and white image that is almost identical to this arcane, leading me to believe that I was in the presence of a deck with strong roots in esoteric knowledge. Over the years, I managed to unravel some of the keys Maritxu left in this card, appreciating the subtleties in the creation of the deck.

Understanding some of these secrets, which are connected to the Basque tradition and the pre-Christian European past, has been a strong incentive to write this book.

This card presents the figure of a male goat with a woman's torso, prominently featuring two female breasts. The head has a double set of goat horns, and a fifth horn emerges from the center, raising a flame. These five horns form an upward-pointing five-pointed star.

In the center of the forehead is a pentacle or inverted five-pointed star. This second pentagram is the dual or complementary to the previous one formed by the horns.

The center of its abdomen is adorned with the caduceus of Hermes. The classic image of two snakes wrapped around a central rod, adopted as a symbol by medicine and used to represent alchemical work in both the East and West. On either side of its waist are the numbers 6 and 0, representing the numerological reduction of XV (1 + 5 = 6 0) in the second decade.

Below the skirt, two hooves are visible, confirming its animal nature, especially in the lower half of its body.

The arms point in opposite directions, the right towards the sky and the left towards the earth. The hands end in a characteristic gesture used for directing energy and blessing in Christianity. The fingers of both arms point to two respective moons. The left arm points to a waxing crescent moon[49], indicating increasing energy favorable for starting endeavors or planting. The moon pointed to by the right arm is waning, a time when energies diminish, suitable for harvesting.

Two large feathered wings extend from the character's body, unlike decks like the Tarot of Marseille, where the devil's wings are leathery, more akin to a bat's and too small for flight.

In the background, on the horizon, there is a house, which could also be a church. At the character's feet, on the right side of the card, is a small green frog. The two chained acolytes present in the Marseille decks are not included in this deck; the image is sufficiently explicit

Aquelarre, Francisco Goya

---

49. In accordance with the position in the Northern Hemisphere of the planet.

and full of content to dispense with them.

The name of the arcane is Aker, which is another difference from its equivalent in other decks, where it is almost always called "The Devil." This enigmatic name was unknown to me for a long time and intrigued me greatly. My first association was with the Egyptian deity of the same name, but its characteristics did not correspond to the image before my eyes. When I learned of Maritxu's nationality, I could make the connection to the Basque Aker.

This discovery opened the door to a deeper understanding of the arcane. The term "aker" has entered Spanish through the word aquelarre, which has a very special origin. In the early 17th century, a series of large-scale inquisitorial trials were held in the Basque Country, perhaps the largest in all of Spain. This process had its epicenter in the village of Zugarramurdi, close to where Maritxu later spent most of her life. In the trial, one of the inquisitors, Juan del Valle Albarado, coined the neologism aquelarre to refer to the gatherings held by the women being judged, in their supposed diabolical practices. Thus, the expression aquelarre is formed by aker = male goat and larre = meadow, referring to the place where the supposed witches' meetings were held.

The spirit or deity is named Akerbeltz, which in Basque is Aker = male goat and beltz = black. This is a typical horned deity and thus connects with Cernunnos, a god from the Celtic tradition, widespread throughout Europe. In both cases, the figure of the male goat represents fertility, the relationship with nature, and its associated cycles.

These pre-Christian deities became a suitable scapegoat to personify evil when triumphant Christianity in Europe wanted to impose itself over the belief systems that preceded it and had persisted until the end of the Middle Ages.

It's interesting to note that many Christian temples were erected on sites of worship of the so-called pagan religions, as pointed out by Murray in "The God of the Witches," referring to the Pillar of the Boatmen, a sculpture discovered in Notre Dame in

1711.

> In the north of Gaul, its importance is manifested in the
> altar discovered beneath the Notre Dame cathedral in
> Paris. The date of the altar is undoubtedly of the Christian
> era; on three sides, there are figures of minor gods repre-
> sented as small beings, and on the fourth side is the head
> of Cernunnos, which is enormous compared to the other
> figures (Murray, 2006).

Therefore, the generalized interpretation given to this card is incomplete if it is only associated with purely negative aspects. I believe that these interpretations reflect an overly ideologized view that rather corresponds to the interests of one religion prevailing over others. A more appropriate meaning is to consider it a reflection on passions and the dangers they entail.

The card itself is a warning about the deep passions and desires that we all have, which are associated with our primal nature. The danger lies in being carried away by these impulses and becoming chained to them, but the solution is not to nullify or repress them because this path leads to the wide range of psychopathologies highlighted by psychoanalysis. The healthier and more productive alternative is to redirect these energies beneficially, as Christine Payne-Towler points out, "This passion and power, frightening but impressive, must be reintegrated into the personality to feed the soul's passage from mortal to immortal" (2006, p. 29).

As previously mentioned, through numerological reduction, this arcane yields VI, as the operation 1 + 5 from XV results in 6. This allows it to be associated with The Lovers, thus revealing the dual nature of the forces warned about by the card's motif.

In the third septenary, the challenge posed by this card is consistent with the level of development and instruction of those who have followed the path laid out by the triumphs. It is no longer the mere containment of passions proposed to the apprentice, but the transmutation of the most visceral desires and passions of those on the path of mastery and aspiring to spiritual transcendence.

The meaning assigned by Martixu Guler in her instruction booklet is as follows: "It is a very bad card. If it appears next to the Consultant, retreat, be prudent in your actions. Ravages, bad intentions, violence, clash, disaster, slavery. Malignant tendency, violation. Disorder, lust. Also marks hidden powers, influence over others, hereditary diseases" (1976, p. 38).

The association of this card is with the Sagittarius sign, the waxing and waning Moon respectively, and the letter ‬ס (samech) of the Hebrew alphabet, linked to fatality.

In this arcane, the relationship with the zodiac sign Sagittarius is very appropriate, as this sign is usually represented by a centaur, with a bow and arrow pointing towards the sky. Centaurs were creatures from Greek mythology with the body of a horse and a human torso from the shoulders.

This mixture represents the nature of Sagittarius, whose lower part is solidly situated in the telluric forces and overwhelmed by its passions. In contrast, the upper, human part looks towards the sky towards elevated, abstract, spiritual matters. This tension characterizes Sagittarius, and resolving it is their great task.

XVI The Tower

This card bears a high degree of similarity to its equivalent in Marseille decks, except for the name, which in the
French version is La Maison Dieu (The
House of God). Perhaps another subtle difference is that the GET version is
more realistic than the Marseille one,
which is drawn with a more comic-like
concept.

The figure represents a tower-shaped
building that is being heavily affected
by a fire and by natural forces in the
form of lightning. As a result of this
disaster, pieces of bricks fall from its
walls, and people are also tumbling
down, some drawn more stylized than
others.

The top of the building is crowned by two small defensive
towers, and from the right one, a person is projected into the distance.

At the bottom of the tower, on its right side, is the number 70, to
represent the numerological operation with XVI ($1 + 6 = 7$). Also,
at the bottom, a door from which a character abruptly emerges.
Above the door, a strange inscription is visible upon close examination, which shows the word AZKAR.

The door is a different element compared to the Marseille deck,
which usually does not show the door, although other traditional
decks like Oswald Wirth do.

The symbolism of the card quickly evokes the Tower of Babel,
a story recounted in the biblical Genesis. This story occurs some
time after the flood in which Noah and his descendants survive.
According to the legend, the earth had been repopulated, and its
inhabitants proposed to build a tower that reached the heavens.

Except for the goal of reaching the heavens, the text does not indicate another purpose for the building, but it is reasonable to assume that after the gigantic flood, its builders wanted it to serve as a refuge in case of a new flood.

Upon seeing the construction, Jehovah considers that if humans had managed to build this tower, there would be nothing they could not achieve. In a peculiar decision, he determines that humans will no longer speak the same language, creating chaos and confusion among them.

At first glance, this decision seems odd, as Jehovah, instead of being pleased with the human capacity demonstrated in building this edifice, sees it as a problem. It's a situation similar to the Fall, where after eating from the tree of knowledge, Jehovah considers that Adam and Eve might also eat from the tree of life and live indefinitely.

I prefer to consider that Jehovah is preventing humans from taking the short or twisted path. The solution of the flood is applied because humanity had reached such a situation that it was no longer possible to continue sustaining it.

Beyond the exegesis that can be made of the biblical scriptures, The Tower, from a symbolic standpoint, refers to a situation that is maintained by ego, caprice, or vanity and comes to an abrupt end. This interruption of the consultant's plans leads to a significant change that upends a substantial part of the affected person's life. However, despite this change, the suggestion posed by the arcane will bring about positive modifications in the consultant's future events, as the base situation is rooted in aspects that imply a significant cost to maintain the situation or project it refers to.

I often say in readings, almost like a mantra that synthesizes the central message of this arcane: "Destruction of a project, but it's positive." Initially, this might seem paradoxical to the listener, but the card confronts us with the opportunity to leave behind situations to which we have been obsessively clinging and that maintaining them is detrimental to our life. The term "project" allows conveying a high level of generalization or abstraction to the event being consulted, which can represent an everyday and concrete situation or something more elaborate like a life choice, adherence to a thought stream, or religious idea.

Like in other arcana, the good witch of Ulía wanted to leave the mark of the lands that saw her birth and were her home for most of her life.

The culture and traditions of the villages in the Basque Country and Navarre are deeply connected to ancestral customs, where the relationship with Mother Nature plays a transcendental role. In this environment of valleys and mountains, close to the Pyrenees, the vision of the Celtiberian peoples managed to survive and left its mark despite attempts to eliminate it. This vision is present in the stories and legends that the author of the deck has captured in some of her arcana.

The inscription on the building's facade gives us the key to understand the message that Maritxu Guler wanted to leave in this arcane, as Azkar is a term from the Basque language referring to a geographical location near Zugarramurdi. This town was the site of a castle, which, of course, was related to the auto-da-fé conducted by the Spanish Inquisition in Zugarramurdi in 1610.

This castle had a tragic history related to the mentioned trials. The garrison had a small detachment of ten soldiers, and one of them, interested in a girl who participated in the sabbaths, was invited to join the sabbat. The soldier attended in the company of the girl, and after returning to his barracks, was punished for his absence with two days of confinement. Upon learning of the punishment, the girl informed the male goat, which, using its arts, managed to make the garrison renounce their military vows so they could celebrate a sabbat inside the castle, a ceremony in which they ended up burning down the fortification.

Since then, the building was known as the haunted castle: askar gaztelu (Altadill, 1883). Beyond the legend, this castle did exist, and press notes from 2009 in Navarra and the Basque Country report excavations that have revealed its perimeter.

The meaning assigned by Guler in her instruction booklet is: "This card announces accident, shipwreck, calamities. Desolation, bankruptcy, misery. Sudden and absolute change. Loss of money, position, love. The Consultant should refrain from rash ventures. Take care of health, there is a risk of accident" (1976, p. 39).

The association of this card is with the letter פ (pe) of the Hebrew alphabet, associated with ruin. This card is assigned to the astrological sign of Capricorn.

XVII The Star

The Star, or El Astro in GET, is an arcane that shows a semi-nude young woman pouring liquids from jars, with one or more stars in the sky.

The GET follows this iconography quite faithfully and introduces some small modifications that mark the distinctive stamp of the author. To begin with, the name of the card is changed from The Star[50] to El Astro. This change introduces the possibility that it refers to the Star of the Magi, as we will see later.

Essentially, the image retains the canonical symbolism in the Marseille deck. The central figure is a nude young woman with a pitcher in each

hand. She is kneeling at the edge of a pond, her right foot inside the water, while the left, on the bent knee, rests on the ground.

The right pitcher, golden in color, pours its liquid into a pond, although the strokes used to draw the water give the idea that it is in motion, which is more consistent with the symbolism of the mixing the girl is performing. The left amphora, white or silver, spills liquid onto the earth.

In the Temperance card, not a single drop is spilled from the jars that the angel is transferring, but in The Star, the young woman is spilling the liquid from both containers; what indicated in the first arcane as a time to gather, to accumulate energy, has now borne fruit and it is time to apply the benefits of the collection.

Above the young woman, in the daytime sky, a star with twenty rays and a pentagram at its center. From the star, a flaming tail that ends in three fine points. At each of these tips are the signs

50. L'Étoile in the Marseille deck.

of Jupiter, Mars, and Saturn, respectively, indicating a possible triple conjunction of these planets.

In the lower part of the star and to the right, the sign of Mercury, and under it, the number 80, indicating the numerological reduction operation of the XVII number of the card for the second decanate.

The central concept associated with this arcane is that of hopeful news, which is encouraging after the disaster warned by The Tower. This concept mainly rests on the symbolism of the star, which makes sense, considering that since time immemorial, in the darkest night and after a storm, if one could look up and spot some stars, it was a sign that the weather was improving.

Among the celestial bodies, there was one special one, its brightness distinguished it from the rest, and it is visible a few hours before the sunrise and also for a few hours before the sunset of the sun: this is Venus. The particularity of being visible shortly before sunrise led to it being called the Morning Star, as it appears shortly before the sunrise as if announcing the end of a long night and the start of a new day.

Venus is associated with the number five and also with the sign ♀, which is commonly used to represent it, and is linked to the five-pointed star or pentagram. The reason for this lies in the fact that a complete cycle of Venus, as observed from Earth, traces this figure in its apparent motion.

This is likely why Maritxu chose the five-pointed star instead of the eight-pointed star seen in the Tarot of Marseille; however, both refer to the planet Venus.

Another association of this arcane is with the Star of Bethlehem, which is believed to have guided the Magi on their journey to greet the birth of Jesus. This is another reason to consider the symbolism of this arcane as related to good news, such as the birth of a spiritual leader and founder of a new religion, based on love for one's fellow beings.

As I previously mentioned, the name change of the card to El

Astro introduces the possibility that, as its name suggests, it refers to a celestial body and not just a star. One of the hypotheses formulated to explain the astronomical phenomenon that led the wise men from the East to Jesus' birth is that it could have been a comet. Consistent with this explanation is the long tail ending in three points present in the star drawn on the card, as comets have this attribute.

However, to leave no stone unturned, this tail ends in three points on which the symbols of Jupiter, Mars, and Saturn are drawn, opening up two explanatory possibilities.

On one hand, with three planets involved, it alludes precisely to what tradition has established as the Three Wise Men. Of the planets mentioned, two are rulers in Greek mythology: Jupiter and Saturn, so they can be considered kings.

Yet, the mention of three planets also opens up the possibility of another hypothesis for the Star of Bethlehem: a planetary conjunction between these three planets. According to astronomy, in the 7th century BC, there was a triple conjunction between Jupiter and Saturn in the sign of Pisces, which for the astrologers of the time must have been a sign of a very important event.

The meaning assigned by Martixu Guler in her instruction booklet is: "Hope. Practical inspiration, idealism. Clarity in projects. Optimism. Favorable omen. Good astrological influence" (1976, p. 40).

The association of this card is with the planet Mercury and with the planets Jupiter, Mars, and Saturn in the three tongues of fire on the star's tail, and with the letter פ (pe) of the Hebrew alphabet associated with hope.

The symbol of Mercury, from an alchemical perspective, is the union of the sign of Venus ♀ with that of Mars ♂, representing the synthesis of the main attributes of these two planets, and primarily, the union of the feminine and the masculine, which is the fundamental achievement of the path proposed by this discipline.

The initials KP, found in the lower right corner of the card, probably allude to Khristóphoros, which literally means "the one who carries Christ." This symbolism could be interpreted as a representation of guidance or bearing a significant message or truth, much like the role of Mercury in mythology as a messenger and guide. This aspect of carrying or conveying important knowledge or insights aligns with the overall theme of The Star (El Astro) as a card of hope, guidance, and the revelation of spiritual or higher truths.

XVIII The Moon

In the Tarot of Marseille, the image of this card was standardized around the depiction of the Moon casting its soft light over two towers, two dogs, and a pond with a lobster.

The GET has maintained the essential elements of the image, introducing small variations that fundamentally preserve the symbolism. The image of the Moon has a strong presence in the card, appearing on the horizon line between two columns. These columns replace the towers seen in the Marseille decks, adding an interesting association with the Strait of Gibraltar.

The Moon is surrounded by rays more reminiscent of solar rays, reminding us that the light source of the satellite orbiting the Earth comes from the Sun. Something similar is found in card number II, The High Priestess, in its upper left corner, where we can see the sun with a face similar to that of the Moon.

In this case, the pond is depicted as a lagoon or sea inlet, extending beyond the strait formed by the position of the columns, with water reaching the horizon line. Another possibility is that it corresponds to the landscape of the famous La Concha beach in San Sebastián, Spain, a familiar landscape for Martixu Guler, even featuring a small island in a position similar to that of the shell in the card.

The Marseille lobster has been changed to a crab, more fitting as it is the figure of this arthropod that is associated with the zodiac sign of Cancer, not the elongated-bodied lobster, even though both belong to the order of decapods.

The two dogs are positioned in front of the lagoon, giving them an appropriate distance from the Moon, which in this deck is located very close to the observer.

At the base of the left column is the zodiac sign of Aquarius, aligned with the shell of an oyster in the middle of the strait. The name of this zodiac sign often leads to misunderstanding, tempting one to associate it with the water element, but the correct association is with the air element to which it is linked.

Twenty-two drops of nocturnal dew are directed towards the Moon, which, through numerological reduction, gives us the number 2+2 = 4. This reminds us of the association this card has with The Emperor, as reflected when placing the cards in septenaries, as both occupy the fourth position of the first and third septenary, respectively (see Illustration number 1).

In the lower left corner, there is a handwritten note that appears to be the date 7-XI-75. Possibly, this is a reminder of a symbolic date for the authors in the creation of the deck. Interestingly, the sum of the digits 1 + 11 + 7 + 5 = 30, which coincides with the number of rays emitted by the Moon in the illustration.

Generally speaking, the image of The Moon invites us to evoke nostalgic and contemplative situations in which we have gazed at this celestial body and shivered at the howling of dogs, seemingly sharing our emotion. The Moon is closely related to our moods and states of mind; its relationship with nature and the accompanying cycles has been known since ancient times.

Since olden days, farmers have known that the best time for sowing is the new moon when the satellite increases its gravitational influence, thereby stimulating the seeds to grow more vigorously. The time for pruning is not during the full moon because at this moment, the plants are brimming with energy, with the sap at the ends of their branches. Therefore, the damage done is greater, and healing takes longer. The appropriate time for pruning is during the waning phase when the Moon's gravitational pull diminishes. At this time, the sap retreats to the center of the plant, so the energy removed is less, and healing is easier.

Animals experience a similar influence in their reproductive and feeding behaviors. Fertilization processes in all types of species are encouraged by the full moon, and knowing that there is greater food availability during this lunar phase, different species prepare for a feast.

This is the case with oysters; they open their shells when the moon rises, as there is a greater availability of plankton at this time. This is likely the reason for including this bivalve in the GET; it can be seen beyond the crab, right in the strait marked by the two columns.

Everything in this arcane speaks of the lunar influence on the inhabitants of planet Earth and the mysteries associated with this phenomenon. It is the realm of emotions and intuition.

The association of the cards with the number to which they are linked, though supported by the symbolism of numbers, may not always seem intuitive, especially for those with higher numerical values. In some cases, numerological reduction clarifies the arcane's relationship with its assigned number, but in others, this relationship remains elusive.

In the case of The Moon, the association with the number 18 is not immediately apparent. However, understanding a specific lunar cycle is helpful in comprehending why this number is assigned to this arcane. This relationship is linked to the Saros cycle, a period it takes for the Moon and the Earth to return to the same positions in their respective orbits. The Saros cycle lasts 18 years and 11 days; thus, an eclipse occurring on a specific date will repeat after this duration.

This cycle has been known since ancient times, possibly as far back as the Chaldean period in the 4th century BCE. It's likely that the early creators of the tarot were aware of this relationship, hence establishing the connection of The Moon with the number 18.

The meaning assigned by Martixu Guler in her instruction booklet is: "Deception. Conspiracy, disillusionment. The truth will be reached but with certain difficulties. Anxious, nostalgic, dark mood" (1976, p. 41).

The association of this card is with the Aquarius sign and with the letter ‫צ‬ (tsade) of the Hebrew alphabet, associated with deception. This association underscores the elusive and often mysterious nature of The Moon, reflecting its influence on our emotions and the subconscious, as well as the often deceptive and confusing aspects of life it can represent.

XVIII The Sun

In the Tarot of Marseille, this arcane is represented by the image of a resplendent Sun dominating the card in its full glory. Like the Moon card, multicolored objects in the shape of drops fall from the star. Below it, two twin children are depicted against a backdrop of a wall.

The GET card faithfully follows the canonical elements and adds to the typical elements with three serpents coiled inside the Sun. The presence of the Sun in this deck is more assertive than in the Marseille decks, occupying a larger portion of the image and incorporating the three mentioned serpents.

Below the Sun are two young females, although with very androgynous characteristics. Their resemblance is striking; they could be twins, which is reinforced by their clothing, as they are dressed in the same way. Unlike the Tarot of Marseille, the two youths are not standing but sitting, and they are not facing the card but are positioned sideways. Another difference from the Marseille decks, regarding the two young figures, is their clothing; in those decks, the children in the image are almost naked, covered only by a small loincloth.

More broadly, the clothing of the two young characters breaks a rule present in the Tarot of Marseille in the third septenary. In that deck, all characters, with the exception of those in La Maison Dieu (The Tower), are naked or almost naked. The GET does not adhere to this convention.

Beyond the young figures, but before the horizon, a crumbled wall or rather a rock replaces the wall present in the Marseille deck.

Between the two youths is a waning crescent moon[51], maintaining the dual balance typical in almost all tarot iconography. Reinforcing this aspect, on the knee of the youth on the left, the sign of Gemini, associated with the air element, is drawn.

Below the Moon, the number 100 is placed, representing the numerological reduction of the card number, which is 19, so 1+9 = 10 or 100 in this arcane, the value of the letter qoph (ק) in the Hebrew alphabet.

From the Sun emanate twenty-three figures shaped like drops or tears. In this case, the number of drops continues the sequence from the Moon card, which contains 22 drops. In The Sun card, the numerological reduction operation yields the number 5 by adding 2+3.

The number five corresponds to the arcane The Hierophant, which is related to The Sun through the septenary system, as both occupy the fifth position in the first and third septenary, respectively (see Illustration 1).

The rays emanating from the Sun in this case exceed those of the Moon by 10 and total 40.

In this card, very similar to the one in the Tarot of Marseille, the most notable deviation from that standard is the presence of three serpents within the Sun. These serpents are coiled around themselves, their heads meeting in the center of the circle they form. The figure they create resembles a triskelion, the typical ornament of Celtic culture, which has provided many beautiful renditions of this icon.

The presence of the serpent within the Sun points to the renewing power of the energy emanating from this star, expressed in the snakes' ability to completely renew their skin. It also establishes a connection with the mythical ouroboros, the circularly arranged serpent biting its own tail, representing the idea of perpetual renewal by self-sustenance.

The card conveys an overwhelming energetic force, indicating a very favorable disposition for all undertakings under its auspi-

---

51. According to how it is visualized in the Northern Hemisphere.

ces. This energy is so positive that even when the card appears reversed in a reading, it doesn't lose its auspicious nature and still represents a positive omen.

In this sense, The Sun differs from other cards in a reading, as when they are reversed, they tend to transform their positive characteristics into their opposite or negative aspects. However, this arcane has such strength and energy that, when placed inverted in a spread, its positive aspects are practically unchanged.

The meaning assigned by Martixu Guler in her instruction booklet is: "Success, happiness, joy. Favorable relationships, blissful union. Achievement, pleasures. Artistic triumphs, awards, and rewards. Reputation, glory, celebrity. Beauty. High-mindedness. Altruism. Conformity to live happily and joyfully" (1976, p. 42).

The association of this card is with the Gemini sign and with the Sun and the waning Moon, and with the letter qoph (ק) of the Hebrew alphabet, associated with happiness.

XX The Cycle

This card presents significant changes compared to the Marseille decks and others. In the Tarot of Marseille, this triumph is represented by three characters, above whom an angel is about to blow the trumpet of the Final Judgment.

In another interpretation, this scene corresponds to the resurrection of Christ at the moment he leaves the tomb, turning his back. The two characters facing forward would be two disciples witnessing the moment, and the angel with his trumpet would be announcing Jesus' resurrection.

Maritxu Guler's choice to represent the symbolism of this triumph is somewhat more abstract, distancing itself from religious imagery and, in a sense, approaching the themes of the New Age movement. The title of the arcane, though it may seem obvious, is the key to understanding the symbolism that the author assigns to this card.

In the card, we can see two suns, one smaller and receding into the distance and another closer and larger. Each of the suns is associated with an astrological sign: the smaller one corresponds to Pisces, and the larger one, to Aquarius.

Beneath the suns, on the earthly surface, there is a building with four columns on its frontispiece and an ankh cross above them on the frontispiece, indicating that it is an initiatory temple.

The number 200 completes the symbolism in the lower-left corner, resulting from the numerological reduction of XX, as 2 + 0 = 200 in the third septenary, and also associated with the Hebrew letter resh (r), which has this number assigned.

The meaning of the card speaks of a change of cycle or stage, which is indicated by the name of the card and the two suns, where one is replacing the other as a result of its evolution. The one that is being left behind is Pisces, and the one replacing it is Aquarius. This motif corresponds to what the New Age movement has popularized as the Age of Aquarius.

According to this concept, humanity would be entering a higher evolutionary phase due to the positive influence that this astrological sign would exert.

The astrological/astronomical background behind this concept is the precession of the equinoxes, a wobbling movement experienced by the Earth's axis in its rotation. This movement, to put it simply52, defines which sign coincides with the spring equinox. When the horoscope was created, this sign corresponded to Aries, and since the Earth's precession movement changes this sign, we are currently in a transitional moment between the signs of Pisces and Aquarius.

This theory, which the author embraces and graphically represents in the drawings on the card, conveys a situation where a change of significant magnitude occurs, enough to be considered epochal. This transformation refers to the spiritual aspects of people, as it is a temple of ancient mysteries that is present in the image, confirmed by the ankh cross at the top of its entrance.

The ankh cross is not the first time it appears in the deck; we saw it at the beginning of the recount of the Major Arcana in the hand of The High Priestess to indicate the generative power associated with this card. Nor is it the first time it is used to identify a building, as it is present in the construction seen behind Death in the thirteenth arcane. In that triumph, the temple is distant, and death is in the foreground, blocking its passage. In The Cycle, the temple is in the foreground, and its access is near.

52.   The explanation for the precession of the equinoxes and its relationship with the zodiac sign is somewhat more complex than what is presented here, but delving deeper into the explanation would not contribute much to the point, where the central theme is an epochal change and, from the perspective of those who propose it, would enable humanity to make an evolutionary leap.

The Lovers, Death, and The Cycle are the penultimate cards in their respective septenaries, representing the stage before completing the teachings at their corresponding level and are possibly the most important challenge of their stage.

In the first septenary, The Lovers pose a choice to the traveler. As presented in the GET, they must choose between virtue and pleasure, between the easy path and the path of transcendence. In the second septenary, Death is the almost insurmountable obstacle that the explorer must overcome in their journey through the arcana if they wish to achieve the balance of Temperance; this is a death almost in the literal sense because the removal of consciousness is so profound that the individual ceases to be who they were to be reborn into a new life. And in the third septenary, the traveled path, the overcome trials allow access to an epochal renewal that is the step before achieving the transcendence of The World. In a sense, this epochal renewal alludes to the time to start returning to others what has been acquired on the spiritual path that has been followed, but maintaining independence of judgment not to tie oneself to these links, in the perspective of the last stage that The World implies.

Maritxu Guler's symbolism in this arcane is interesting. Once again, as in other arcana, she eludes Christian or indirectly Christian symbolism. She does this very clearly in: The High Priestess, The Hierophant, and The Devil, and more elusively in: The Hanged Man, The Tower (as La Maison Dieu), and The Star. The only exception to Maritxu's choice is in Justice, where she introduces a Christian theme with the incorporation of King Solomon. And with all the richness incorporated in The Judgment card of the Tarot of Marseille, it was not easy to find an alternative motif that adequately expressed the symbolism required by the card.

In the Marseille Tarot decks, The Judgment card is depicted in a very compelling manner, suggestively preparing for the transcendence of The World. Both interpretations given to this arcane – the Final Judgment or the Resurrection of Christ – are apt for continuing the journey to The World card.

The Final Judgment speaks of the Second Coming of Christ and is the moment of resurrection of all the dead to be judged, with the final destiny of all souls being decided for eternity. A dramatic account of this event can be found in the Book of Revelation:

> 12 And I saw the dead, great and small, standing before the throne, and books were opened. Another book was opened, which is the book of life. The dead were judged according to what they had done as recorded in the books. 13 The sea gave up the dead that were in it, and Death and Hades gave up the dead that were in them, and each person was judged according to what they had done. 14 Then Death and Hades were thrown into the lake of fire. The lake of fire is the second death. 15 Anyone whose name was not found written in the book of life was thrown into the lake of fire. (Revelation 20:12-15).

The other interpretative option I mentioned – the Resurrection of Christ – is a highly significant episode in Christian tradition. This occurs on the third day after Jesus' death, following his crucifixion. After lying in the tomb provided by Joseph of Arimathea, Jesus returns to life from his stay among the dead. In this return, which lasts for forty days, he completes the teaching of the apostles and then departs permanently, having completed his earthly mission.

Whichever card number XX is chosen, whether from the Tarot of Marseille or the GET, each with its distinct motifs and ways of representing this stage of spiritual development, the choice is appropriate, as both speak of a pivotal moment when a stage is completed and concluded, leading to an inner transformation that enables transcendence.

The meaning assigned by Martixu Guler in her instruction booklet: "It is the omen of an absolute change of position, for better or for worse. One must not fall asleep in laziness or forgetfulness. We have a mission to fulfill. Providence will reveal it to us, be prepared for when the call is made" (1976, p. 43).

The association of this card is with the signs Pisces and Aquarius, representing the transition from one era to another, and with the planet Saturn and the letter resh (ר) of the Hebrew alphabet, linked to renewal.

The Fool

In the Tarot of Marseille, this card represents a festive character, a jester, chosen to embody the spirit of a carefree and joyful journey. Adorned in a multicolored outfit, he carries a knapsack tied to a staff over his right shoulder and holds a stick in his right hand. A peculiar hat sits atop his head, and behind him, an animal resembling a cat tears at his right pant leg, seemingly without bothering him. His face is youthful, with a sparse, pointed beard, and his garments are red, blue, and yellow – the primary colors – giving him a striking and cheerful appearance.

The GET's depiction of The Fool retains the essence of the traditional symbolism but introduces some interesting modifications worthy of detailed analysis.

The character illustrated in the card is a young, blonde man with a short beard. His body and face appear human, but his ears end in points, and two small horns protrude from the front of his head. His head is topped with a curious conical hat with vertical colored stripes, adorned with ribbons at the tip.

Unlike the Marseille deck, where the staff is supported over the right shoulder, he carries a knapsack hanging from a staff over his left shoulder. In his right hand, he holds a corn cob.

He is dressed in furs that end at his knees, leaving parts of his legs exposed. Around his waist, three bells jingle with the movement of his body as he walks.

While his clothing is not as colorful as in the Marseille Tarot, due to the furs, the knapsack and the hat on his head provide the necessary color to make the character stand out.

An undefined animal, the size of a cat, bites his right leg, seemingly without much effect on him.

His attitude is cheerful and carefree, to the extent that his left foot steps over the edge of a slope seemingly without him noticing it.

The character chosen by Martixu Guler for this card is again a figure from Basque-Navarrese tradition, identifiable as Zanpantzar[53], a traditional Basque character who announces the start of carnival by ringing his bells. He typically wears a sheepskin vest over his shoulders and waist, colorful handkerchiefs, several bells around his waist, and a conical hat on his head with ribbons at the tip. There are local variants in some towns with minor differences.

The character's nature is festive, hence his participation in the carnival. With the bells, he scares away evil spirits and, following winter, announces and forces the awakening of nature.

The usual meaning of this card is of someone detached from material aspects and conventions, with enough flexibility to embark on a journey leaving everything behind without care. From a more transcendental perspective, the person beginning this journey is prepared to let their ego die to be reborn into a new life, which involves emptying consciousness and making room for new experiences without the prejudices of a previous life.

Therefore, in all tarot decks, the chosen figure is that of a jester or someone from the medieval-renaissance culture, embodying these characteristics to adorn the card.

The placement of The Fool card is controversial in all decks, as it is not numbered, and there is a convention to place it either at the beginning or the end of the Major Arcana. It can even take the place of any of the cards, due to the flexibility characteristic of the character. For this reason, it is accepted that The Fool is the precursor to the joker or wild card in English decks.

53.   The origin of the name Zanpantzar is unknown, although some believe it is related to a medieval French character named Saint Pansard, which translated into Spanish means the saint of the belly.

In some villages, this character is called Joaldunak.

However, in the case of the GET, the controversial aspect is additional, as the numbering of the cards is interrupted at XX with The Cycle card and resumes with The World at XXII, leaving out the number XXI. The Fool does not carry this number but is marked with 300, resulting from its association with the letter shin (w) of the Hebrew alphabet, as this letter has this value in that code, especially in Kabbalah. The Cycle and The World cards are associated with the numbers 200 and 400, respectively, due to the Hebrew letters corresponding to them.

Because of these numerical relationships, it is natural to place The Fool between The Cycle and The World. Additionally, the position of the letter shin (ש) is twenty-first in the Hebrew alphabet. This placement of The Fool situates this deck in the Kabbalistic correspondence system known as Gra, which, as mentioned earlier, corresponds to the oldest version of the Kabbalistic doctrine.

The meaning assigned by Martixu Guler in her instruction booklet is: "Madness, thoughtlessness, extravagance. Folly. Ridiculous acts. Obsession. Frivolity. Complete abandonment" (1976, p. 45).

The association of this card is with the letter shin (ש) of the Hebrew alphabet, linked to expiation. According to the Gra system of Kabbalistic correspondences, it is associated with the element of fire.

XXII The World

The last of the Major Arcana is also one of the most symbolically rich. In the Tarot of Marseille, a feminine or androgynous figure is depicted, nude and casually covered by a band that only hides the genitals. The character is surrounded by a garland of flowers, and on the exterior, in four positions, it is encircled by four beings, three of them animals and the fourth an angel.

The number assigned to the card is XXI, the last and highest in this series of arcana. Remember that in the Marseille decks, The Fool is not numbered.

The variations introduced by Maritxu Guler in this arcane are very minor and do not substantially alter the essential elements. The most significant change is in the number, which in this deck is XXII. The arcane preceding it in Roman numerals is The Cycle, which has XX, leaving XXI vacant, suggesting, as mentioned before, that this position corresponds to The Fool.

Reinforcing the argument given in the previous arcane, it should be noted that The Fool does not have a Roman numeral, but in Arabic numerals, it is marked with 300, placing it between the 200 of The Cycle and the 400 of The World. These three Arabic numerations, 200, 300, and 400, are assigned to the values of the respective Hebrew letters associated with each arcane.

The other variation corresponds to the central figure, which in this case is clearly androgynous, having drawn male genitals and female breasts. Although the latter are covered by a band, they are distinctly feminine.

The general symbolism of the figure derives from the Pantocrator, an image from medieval art representing Christ surrounded by the four evangelists: Luke, Matthew, Mark, and John, either directly or through the four symbolic beings representing them: an angel, an eagle, a bull, and a lion.

Pantocrator is a term from Greek meaning 'all-powerful', with 'pan' meaning 'all' and 'crator' sharing a root with 'cracy' as in 'democracy', meaning 'powerful'.

The image typically depicts Christ with the right hand making the gesture of blessing and the left hand holding a book.

This figure can be seen in many medieval and Gothic churches and in the pictorial art adorning their interiors.

In some cases, the figure of Christ is accompanied by the four evangelists in human appearance or according to their symbolic representation in the four aforementioned beings.

Another characteristic element in these representations is a decorative item resembling a garland, shaped like a mandorla. This term comes from Italian and means 'almond'. It was used as a frame or halo to enclose the figure of Christ or other characters considered sacred in Christianity.

The mandorla or Vesica Piscis (Latin for 'fish bladder') is a figure obtained by intersecting two circles so that the circumference of one coincides with the center of the other, in other words, they share the same radius. The common figure for both circles corresponds to the Vesica Piscis.

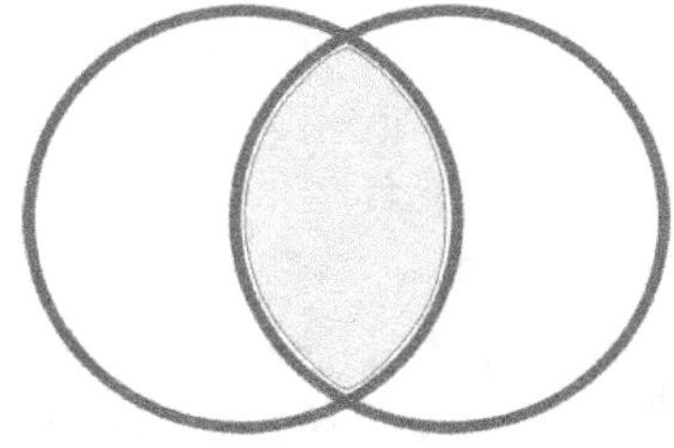

The symbolism of this figure is extensive, and for our purpose, it is worth noting that the relationship between its height and width is 265/153 = 1.73203, which is an approximation of √3 (square root of three).

Among other curiosities, the number 153 corresponds to the number of fish in the miracle of the fishes, according to the Gospel of John (John 21:11).

For these and other reasons, this figure is considered to have sacred proportions and is used in religious art to frame characters considered holy. It is used in the Pantocrator to surround the figure of Christ in majesty.

An image in which a character is surrounded by four beings is known as a tetramorph, from the Greek τετρα, tetra, "four," and μορφη, morphē, "form." The first precedent of such a figure is the vision of Ezekiel (Ezekiel 1:10), where the Old Testament prophet describes having seen four beings with "...the face of a man, and the face of a lion on the right side of all four, and the face of an ox on the left side of all four, and also the face of an eagle among all four."

Another relevant vision of this type is mentioned in Revelation, the last book of the Bible. It states:

> Surrounding the throne, and on each side of the throne,
> are four living creatures, full of eyes in front and behind: 7
> the first living creature like a lion, the second living crea-
> ture like an ox, the third living creature with a face like
> a human face, and the fourth living creature like a flying
> eagle. (Revelation 4:6-8)

In the Pantocrator represented in cathedrals, the figure of Christ appears making the gesture of blessing with his right hand and holding a book in his left, most likely referring to the character mentioned in the biblical book of Revelation.

All these elements show us the figure of Christ realized, having completed his earthly mission and ruling from the heavens, and this is the image that the World arcane captures: that of realization. The mystical journey that The Fool began, starting with

The Magician, completes its cycle in The World, where it finds its consummation.

Between these two cards, The Magician and The World, there are very clear similarities in the Tarot of Marseille, which are somewhat attenuated in the GET due to Maritxu Guler's choice to represent the first arcane with the figure she depicts on the card. However, the most significant aspects of these similarities are maintained.

The Magician in the Marseille Tarot has on his table the four elements that make him a creator, and these four elements have an earthly, pure, primordial character. In The World, the four beings that surround the central figure are present, but they no longer correspond to the earthly world; they are beings that have transcended this world. In the GET, the four elements do not occupy the same space as in the Marseille deck. The author preferred to deliver the image of a human being with a celestial map with the seven planets drawn on their body, as a guide for spiritual development, but the four elements are still present in the ankh cross that the character holds in their right hand.

The Consultant holds a wand in his left hand, raised towards the sky, and his right hand points towards the earth, indicating that he serves as a bridge between both. In The World, the central character holds the same wand as The Magician, but in their right hand, and both hands are raised towards the sky, indicating that their condition belongs to this sphere.

Within the laurel mandorla, the Sun and the crescent Moon54 are present, in a clear allusion that the alchemical weddings have been completed, which explains and reinforces the androgynous nature of the character.

Another symbolic aspect that complements the meaning of this triumph is the theory of the four elements used from Classical Antiquity to the Renaissance. In this theory, the creation of the universe is explained through four basic elements: water, air, earth, and fire. Different philosophers considered water, air, earth, or fire as the primary element, without consensus among them.

---

54.   As seen from the northern hemisphere of the planet.

Aristotle, in turn, held that these four elements were earthly and corruptible and that, therefore, the stars, i.e., the celestial world, must be formed by a fifth element, whose characteristics would be immobile, unchangeable, subtle, eternal, and he called this element quintessence or ether.

The nature of the motion of this fifth element is circular, unlike the other four elements, which is rectilinear. This theory, which was discarded at the beginning of the 20th century with the development of modern physics, has begun to regain strength with theories seeking to explain dark energy. According to the latest research, this form of energy makes up 70% of the existing matter-energy in the universe and causes a repulsive gravitational force that explains the expansion of the universe.

When closely observed, The World card shows the four beings surrounding the central figure, each taking on the characteristic appearance assigned to the four elements, symbolized by a square, representing the form of matter. In contrast, the central character, which we can associate with the quintessence or the celestial world, is surrounded by an oval or circular figure, confirming that their nature is not of this world but has transcended the material world and, therefore, exists on a different, spiritual plane. The central character is, consequently, the result of the transcendence of the four elements, the overcoming of the material world.

The meaning assigned to this card by Martixu Guler in her instructional booklet is: "Reward, perfection, achievement. The final and happy result of all work and effort. Satisfaction. Capability. Success in exams, in business, in inventions. Physical and psychic strength. Good health" (1976, p. 44).

The association of this card is with the planet Jupiter and the letter ת (tau) of the Hebrew alphabet, associated with reward.

The four beings surrounding the central figure, as we have seen, are related to the symbolism of the four elements, and it is not coincidental that this metaphor is present in the last of the major arcana. As we will see, the minor arcana are organized into four groups of sixteen cards, and thus The World card introduces the key symbolism for their understanding.

The key to understanding the minor arcana, as well as their main relationships, is found in the following summary table.

Being	Astrological Sign	Evangelist	Element
Angel	Aquarius	Matthew	Water[55]
Eagle	Scorpio	John	Air
Lion	Leo	Mark	Fire
Bull	Taurus	Luke	Earth

55. This correspondence is of a more naturalistic order: angel-water, lion-fire, bull-earth, eagle-air. There are alternative correspondences where the relationship between the angel and the eagle is switched, so it is associated: angel-air, eagle-water.

Spreads

In the initial section of the book, we announced that a fundamental component of tarot was its relational nature. I even proposed a theoretical framework like the General Systems Theory to update this ancient tradition with the new tools offered by science. However, so far, we have not witnessed the magic in action. I was careful in examining each of the cards and presented them in their context. The tool of the septenaries guided us in investigating the arcana, and I believe that by now, the reader is anticipating how this proposal translates concretely into reading and interpretation.

A tarot deck can be used in multiple ways, among others as a tool for personal reflection and reading. In this process, the cards provide a means for the consultant to clarify aspects that concern or draw attention in their life.

The reading can follow two paths:

- A systematic one, where the cards have a certain interrelation between them, serving as a guide for the reader.

- A spontaneous one: here, the reader does not use systematic tools but lets their intuition guide them in the reading.

At first glance, there seems to be a value judgment in this classification, but that is not the case. Both options are perfectly valid and have similar levels of complexity and difficulty in learning.

These two reading alternatives are apparently opposed, but the truth is that they are not, and most tarot readers use a combination of them. However, for clarity of exposition for the reader, I have chosen to separate them.

From a pedagogical perspective, learning the systematic option lends itself more easily to a logical and rational approach, and therefore, is within reach of a written medium like this one.

The spontaneous alternative requires the development of intuition and the reader's perceptual skills. Some of these can be learned through a book, but the essence of such a method is more easily transmitted through orality. The face-to-face relationship with someone who guides the learner is almost irreplaceable. Therefore, I have chosen not to delve into this alternative in this medium and focus on the exposition of the systematic method.

In systematic reading, spreads acquire paramount importance and are the preferred alternative for those who follow this option. A spread is an arrangement of cards according to a pre-established layout, in which each card fulfills a function to facilitate reading.

One of the advantages of a spread is that it expands the possibilities already inherent in the cards, as assigning meaning to the positions in the arrangement combines with the meaning of the cards.

A second advantage of using a spread is that it facilitates the reader's work by placing them in a familiar routine, which they can comfortably follow. With practice, this habit will allow them to perform the more mechanical aspects effortlessly and concentrate on those aspects that interest them.

Another advantage of using a spread is that it can be associated with a ritual. By this, I mean a set of procedures that help create the right mood and disposition for both the consultant and the interpreter of the reading.

There is a great diversity of spreads, and the reader should choose one that suits them. Therefore, it is advisable that in their initial experiences, they try out a few to see which one facilitates their interpretive work the best.

Some spreads are very old and could be called classic, almost a "must" for those starting in tarot reading. Others are more recent creations. In recent years, there has been a proliferation of spreads, which have been shared through modern communication means. Among this numerous and creative set of spreads, some are frankly outlandish and can be disregarded. But this is a matter of personal choice, and the reader should choose according to their convenience.

In this work, I will focus on a spread that is especially relevant for the deck, which is based on the configuration of a star to lay out the cards: the seven-pointed star spread, or Siebenstern.

Preliminarily, I will present some classic or traditional spreads that will contribute to the reader's training and provide the necessary context for an adequate understanding of the seven-pointed star spread. Among the most well-known, we can mention the following:

- The three-card spread.

- The cross spread.

- The Celtic cross spread.

Three-card spread.

This spread is a simple way to obtain a tarot reading. It is one of the simplest and most useful. Generally, three cards are selected, representing the past, present, and future of the consultant. The past card is placed to the left of the reader, the present card in the middle, and the future card to the right.

Alternatively, and complementarily to these assigned values, the left card can represent what is against the consultant's question. The right card, in this case, represents what is in favor, what facilitates the question. And the middle card represents the question itself.

In this example, viewed from the perspective of the reader, The Master represents the past of the person consulting, The Chariot of Hermes the present, and The Two Paths, the future.

Pasado   Presente   Futuro

The usual procedure for carrying out this spread involves asking the consultant to cut the deck and then laying out the cards from the top of the pile, covered.

First, the card corresponding to the past is turned over and interpreted, followed by the card for the present, and finally, the card for the future. With all three cards revealed, a complementary interpretation of the first two can be made, and then a synthesis is formulated.

This spread is sometimes complemented by drawing an additional card for the past and another for the future, which adds more information. These two additional cards can be included from the beginning or revealed after the first three cards have been interpreted to further complement the reading.

Cross Spread

In this spread, the cards are laid out with the first four forming a cross and the fifth in the middle.

The consultant cuts the deck, allowing the cards to be laid out from the top, in the following order.

The first card is placed to the left in position 1, the second to the right in position 2, and so on, until the fifth card, which is placed in the middle of the other four.

The values assigned to the positions are:

1. Affirmation, in favor. This card suggests what should be done, as it is related to the favorable aspects for the consultant. It presents their behavior, way of acting, merits, friendships, and what inspires confidence.

2. Denial, against. The card in this position represents what opposes the consultant's aspirations. It's a warning of danger and what should be avoided, as it only brings problems.

3. Discussion, judgment. The third card presents the path to follow, clarifying the stance that should be established.

4. Solution, verdict. The fourth position anticipates the result, evaluating the pros and cons that intervene for or against the consultant.

5. Synthesis. Finally, the card in the fifth and key position communicates the vital theme, as everything rests on it. It is the fundamental aspect of the consulted problem. It symbolizes the consultant, as this card provides the key to their question.

There are some variations to this spread, as we will see next, but essentially, all maintain a similar structure.

Oswald Wirth's Version of the Cross Spread

Oswald Wirth's variant, as presented in his book "The Tarot of the Magicians" (1990b), differs in the method of selecting the cards, but otherwise is similar to the previous method.

For the selection of cards, Wirth applies a strictly numerological procedure as follows:

First, the cards are shuffled, and then the consultant is asked to choose a number less than twenty-three. The chosen number corresponds to the first card, counting the cards from the top of the deck. Then a number less than twenty-two is requested. This continues in the same manner until the fourth card.

For the fifth card, the procedure changes, as this one is obtained by adding the digits corresponding to the first four cards. If the number is higher than eighteen, the digits of the resulting number are added together. The number for the fifth card must be less than eighteen, as these are the cards remaining in the deck: Once the number for the card is obtained, it is placed in the middle of the cross.

For example, if the first four cards obtained are: The Master V, The Chariot of Hermes VII, The Two Paths VI, and The World XXII, the following operation is carried out:

$$5 + 7 + 6 + 2 + 2 = 22 = 2 + 2 = 4$$

Thus, the fifth card will be in position number four, counting from the top of the deck.

Celtic Cross Spread

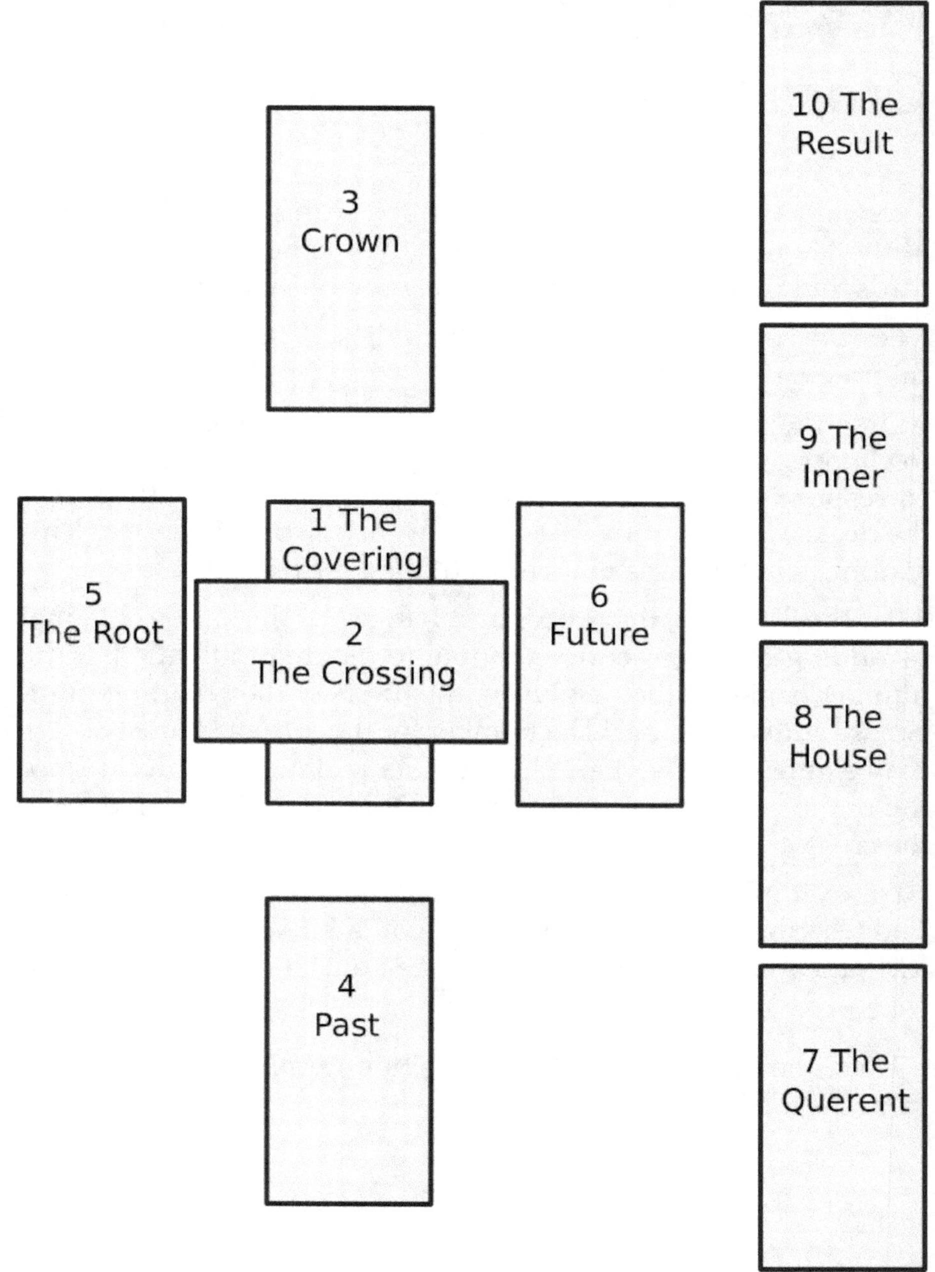

This spread is frequently used by many card readers due to its medium level of difficulty. It requires ten cards and can be performed using only the Major Arcana or, for those familiar with the complete deck, all 78 cards.Its versatility lies in the number of cards used and their arrangement, making it suitable for all types of questions and situations. The additional cards beyond the simple cross allow for an expanded reading, deepening the understanding of aspects where the querent may have doubts.

To execute the spread, the cards are laid out according to their numbered order. The interpretation focuses on the first six cards, which play a central role in the reading. The next four cards, from 7 to 10, support and elaborate on the explanation of the first six.

1. The Covering: This card represents the current situation of the querent, the theme of the spread, or the starting point of the narrative.

2. The Crossing: The second card, placed across the first, represents what is crossing or intermingling with the current situation. It's not necessarily against the situation but what's involved in the context of the inquiry.

3. The Crown: The querent's awareness or perception of the situation. It reflects what is recognized about the issue or potentially what is aimed for.

4. The Past: This refers to the foundation of the question, underlying factors that are present in the querent's life.

5. The Root: Complementing the previous card, this shows deeper aspects or causes that have led to the current situation.

6. The Future: What is likely to happen next. It's the immediate future and should be revisited when interpreting the last card of the spread.

7. The Querent: Represents the person consulting the cards and is the first of four cards that add depth to the initial interpretation.

8. The House: How others see the querent or the environment where the situation occurs. More generally, it's the context of the posed question.

9. The Inner Self: The querent's expectations, hopes, or fears are reflected in this card. While it might not provide oracular information, it helps the querent clarify their view of the situation.

10. The Outcome: Offers a long-term perspective on the issue and should be analyzed in combination with the 6th card, as both provide a view of the future. However, the latter presents a more trend-based perspective.

As seen, this spread offers a wider range of possibilities than the previous ones examined and, when applied flexibly, provides great versatility to any tarot reader who becomes familiar with it.

Gran Tarot Esotérico Spread[56]

After discussing some traditional spreads, we can now focus on one that is essentially included in the Gran Tarot Esotérico: the Seven-Pointed Star Spread.

This image is incorporated into the back of the cards and corresponds to a very old arrangement of astrological symbolism. For more details on this aspect, refer to the section "Structure of the GET" and Illustration 4, where the origin of this symbolism is

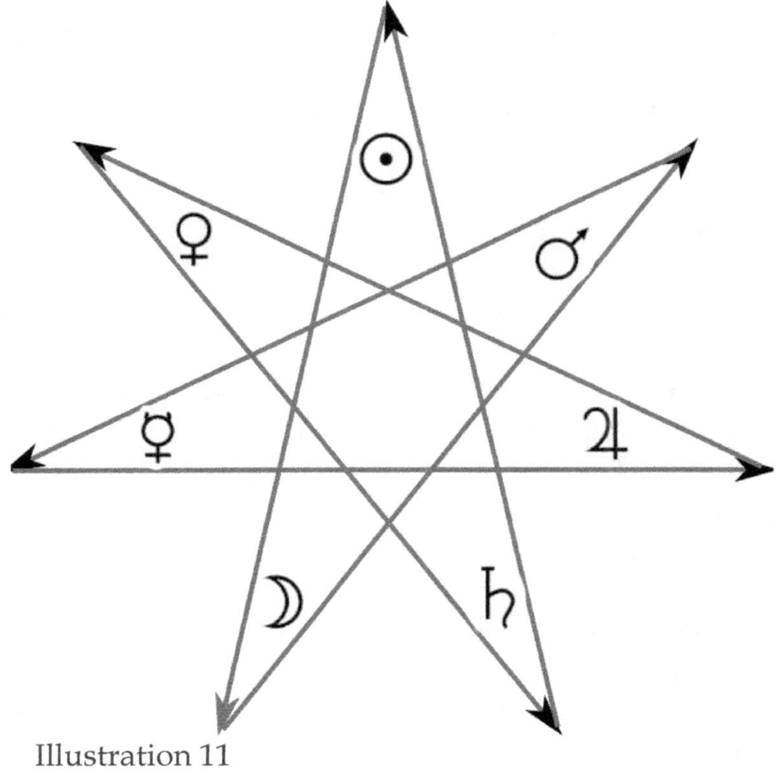

Illustration 11

---

56. This spread is inspired by the symbolism of the GET (Gran Tarot Esotérico), but it has been developed by me, the author. Therefore, I am responsible for any inaccuracies it may contain.

explained in detail.

As mentioned in that section, based on the seven-pointed star and the image represented in the "El Consultante" card, I developed a reading system that arranges the cards in the form of a seven-pointed star. Each point is assigned an area of the person's life defined by the planet in that position. Furthermore, each point, through the planet, relates to the position of the body where this planet is located in the human figure of the "El Consultante" card. In Illustration 11, we have, as a scheme, the star that is found in the central part of the back of the cards, which was presented in Illustration 2. Here, the essentials of this image are retained: the seven-pointed star, the planets according to their location on each of the rays, and a sequence suggested by the ends of the arrows.

The star, according to the diagram in this figure, provides the basic structure for the spread, as the cards are placed on it. The planets, in turn, define the area of the person's life in relation to the card placed in a specific spread.

According to my ritual[57], the querent selects a card from the deck, places it on top of the deck, and the deck is cut again. Cards are then spread out at the points of the arrows until the card selected by the querent appears, which is placed in the center of the star.

The sequence in which the cards are spread starts with the position of the Sun and follows the order suggested by the arrows in Illustration 11.

Once the complete layout is obtained, the interpretation begins. I unfold the cards face up from the beginning, as this allows me to quickly form an impression by looking at the set of cards, which is very useful.

The value assigned to each position in the star is a combination of the symbolism associated with each planet according to astrology and the area of the body where that pla-

---

57. Explaining the ritual in detail is not relevant here, as in many aspects it is personal to each tarot reader and it is often better transmitted through oral tradition.

net[58] is located in the "El Consultante" card.

As mentioned in the section "Origin of the Gran Tarot Esotérico", the figure that appears in this card is probably based on the Man of Gichtel, a set of images that appear in Johan Georg Gichtel's book "Teosophia Práctica", with which it has extraordinary similarity.

In this figure, the seven planets of astrology are inscribed in a human figure and connected by a spiral that starts from the heart, where the Sun is located, to the head, where Saturn is situated.

The planets are located in the body according to the positions assigned to the chakras in the Hindu system, differing only in that Gichtel's image does not present the root chakra located in the genitals. Consequently, the image of "El Consultante" also does not represent this energy center.

The presence of the planets connected by a spiral in a human figure is a beautiful allusion to the relationship between the microcosm and the macrocosm, and the image of "El Consultante" makes this connection, practically serving as a guide or body map to the celestial world for those beginning with this deck. This link suggests that the human being is a small universe and not just in a generic or almost metaphysical way, as some esoteric groups or the New Age movement tend to do, but in a concrete way, since our body and our consciousness are organized according to the same laws that structure the macrocosm.

This metaphor is so precise that modern medicine and psychology account for it through the way biology operates in our organism and the way we internalize the product of our social relationships in a bodily manner. Certainly, the inverse is also true, that is, how we externally express our moods and emotions bodily[59].

---

58. It's important to remember that of the seven celestial bodies represented in the star, only five are planets according to modern astronomical classification, and the other two, the Sun and the Moon, are luminaries, as defined by astrology.

59. This aspect should be considered by every tarot reader who wants to progress, as among the skills in which they must improve is the abili-

Combining the two aspects explained above: the star on the back of the cards and the representation of the seven planets inscribed in the body of "El Consultante", I have constructed an assignment of the areas of life of the person associated with each of the planets. According to mythology and astrology, planets influence or govern aspects of life, hence this association is possible.

The associations established by astrology and mythology have been adjusted with the position occupied in the body of "El Consultante" and the energy center associated with it. In this way, the system is made coherent as a whole. For instance, Saturn is associated by some authors with characteristics such as heavy or hard and thus linked to the earth, but in the body of "El Consultante," it is located in the head, more precisely in the crown, so it is more appropriate to relate it to transcendent experiences or spirituality. For greater precision, I will indicate in the description of each planet the respective correction.

According to the symbolism indicated, the planets present the following characteristics:

Sun

The Sun (☼) is Apollo in Rome (Helios in Greece), the Sun god. The sun, as the ruler and source of all activities, naturally assumes a strong predominance in a person's activities. It can be said that it directs and guides a person's actions, as the Sun, occupying the position of the heart, forms the internal structure of the person.

The place this star occupies in the body of "El Consultante" is the central position, the chest, and the point where the spiral connecting it to the other planets begins. This location has led me to give it two functions. On one hand, it is considered the guiding or secondary card in the spread, as the main card is the one selected by the consultant. On the other hand, its position in

---

ty to perform a good body reading, as well as, in general, to strengthen their communicative abilities. A good tarot reading takes advantage of all the communicational interaction that occurs between the consultant and the tarot reader.

the location of the heart has made me associate it with love in a universal sense, not strictly in a romantic context. It's about detachment and generosity towards others.

The energy radiated by the Sun is powerful, thus enhancing the attributes of the card that falls in this position. This energy permeates everything it touches, helping to bring things to light, thus serving as a guide to the choice made by the consultant.

The clarity of the star reinforces the ability to discern and helps perceive with wisdom. Therefore, if there are unclear aspects during the reading, it is always a good option to refer to the card in this position in the spread.

The placement of the Sun in the star reaffirms these options, as it is located at the top vertex, from where it dominates all other stars at the remaining six ends.

Moon

The Moon (☽) is associated with Diana in Rome (Selene in Greece or Artemis). She is a Moon goddess or goddess of the hunt.

Unlike the Sun, the Moon reigns at night where it reaches all its splendor and precedes the other planets that usually follow it in its nocturnal appearance. It illuminates variably and thus uncertainly. In this sense, it escapes the dictates of logic and delves into the world of intuition and dreams.

Sensitivity, imagination, intuition, and even clairvoyance are attributes that this position will enhance in the card placed in it.

In the figure of "El Consultante", the Moon is located in the abdominal area, more precisely in the lower belly. It is the place of the uterus and its homologous organ, the prostate, and therefore, it is a position associated with fertility, family, and by extension, the home.

Remember that the Moon regulates tides and many biological cycles, including female menstruation. The nature of this star leads to a complementary and dual relationship with the Sun, making it advisable to interpret the cards in these positions together.

Again, the star confirms this placement, situating it in the lower left vertex.

Mars

Mars ($\male$) is related to Mars in Rome (Ares in Greece). He is the god of war in the classical world but is also associated with strength, dynamism, virility, among other attributes (Perajordi, 1980). A great lover, mythology attributes more than thirty children to him. Among his preferred partners was Aphrodite (Venus in Rome).

Unlike Venus, which symbolizes passive love, the love of Mars is active, magnetic, animalistic. This view of mythology is confirmed by astrology, which considers the influence of this planet as opposite (or complementary) to that of Venus.

The position Mars occupies in the body of "El Consultante" is the throat, and this location has led me to assign this area in the spread to the social relations of the person consulting the cards. I understand this assignment might seem somewhat arbitrary, given the tendency to associate the influence of this planet with conflicts, distancing it from relating to a person's socialization. However, considering the faculties that the chakra system assigns to the throat, I incline towards this option.

According to the Hindu system, the throat chakra enables faculties associated with sound, including the voice. Let me illustrate this concept with a story from Middle Earth. According to Tolkien in his book "The Two Towers" from "The Lord of the Rings" trilogy, Saruman is a character from the same fraternity of wizards as Gandalf the Grey. Saruman is described as possessing deep wisdom and power over people's minds. His skill lies in his voice, capable of enchanting crowds and, when conversing alone with him, he has the ability to convince you of almost anything.

In this example from literature, Tolkien clearly illustrates the faculties associated with this energy center, and it inclined me to assign it to social relationships, to a person's friendly bonds. To reinforce the argument, I can say that a "Martian" attitude can predispose us to generate potential conflicts with our closest ones.

Venus

Venus (♀) in Rome (Aphrodite in Greece). Goddess of love, associated with fertility and enthusiasm.

This planet is the antithesis of Mars. In Venus, we find qualities that make life enjoyable, including delight, beauty, joy, love, softness, and happiness. The inclination for embellishment and seduction in its influence can lead to lightness and even frivolity, among the negative aspects of its influences.

"El Consultante" places this planet in the area below the heart, and thus I associate it with aspects related to partnership and romantic matters. The card that falls in this position in the spread is key when the question or concerns of the consultant are related to these types of matters and should be the second in importance after the central card if the question addresses romantic or partnership themes.

On the other hand, if the issue is related to fertility or children, I give more importance to the card located in the Moon, although the card in Venus will also provide guidance on this topic.

Mercury

Mercury (☿) in Rome (Hermes in Greece) is the messenger of the gods in Greek culture, in his equivalent version as Hermes.

The Roman civilization attributes to the Greek god characteristics such as: messenger of the gods and thus a role of communicator, and assigns him an important role in commerce. From an etymological perspective, Mercury is rooted in the Latin expression "merx," meaning merchandise.

The characteristics attributed to it by traditional astrology are movement, liveliness, and constant activity. According to this view, its main influence on humans is expressed in the nervous system and the brain. The influence of Mercury on individuals makes them adaptable people (Perajordi, 1980). The vivacity and diversity of this planet's influence have the downside of a certain tendency towards superficiality, indecision, and dispersion.

In the card "El Consultante," Mercury is located between Venus and the Moon, in the position where the kidney-associated chakra would be.

The aforementioned set of associations inclined me to assign the economic activities of individuals and, by extension, activities in general. The word that best fits this concept is the English expression "business."

Jupiter

Jupiter (♃) in Rome (Zeus in Greece) is the father and leader of the gods. Though he shares functions and attributes with Zeus, he does not derive directly from him as other gods of the pantheon do; in his case, he comes directly from the indigenous peoples of Rome, like the Etruscans. From an etymological perspective, the Latin expression "Iuppiter" comes from Indo-European roots, where "dyu" means light and "piter" father, so the name of the god would mean "father of light."

Astrology assigns the influence of this planet to everything that is ascending, regulating the leading thought in humans. Consciousness, justice, and wise reign are also inherent to it.

The placement of this planet in the card "El Consultante" confirms the above, as it is located at the brow chakra. The Hindu chakra system assigns this energy center to what is called the powers of light, meaning vision. Traditional systems consider that the powers associated with this level are so significant that practitioners usually succumb to the power and end up using it for their own benefit.

The role of the god Jupiter in the Roman pantheon, as well as the powers associated with the energy center where the planet is located, has led me to attribute power as the area of life of the person in this sphere. I am aware that this sphere of influence may not seem so evident, but we all move in a series of relationships where this dimension of human interactions is present, whatever the area in which it is expressed. It could be our center of work, academic, or social activity; in all of them, we enter into a dynamic of interactions in which we are exposed to relate to others in a way where power is operating.

Saturn

Saturn ($\hbar$) in Rome (Kronos in Greece) is the god of duty, punishing those who do not fulfill their responsibilities properly.

Astrology assigns to this planet, the farthest of those known by the ancients, properties of stability, inertia, regularity, and precision. From an intellectual point of view, it orients towards deep reflection and methodical and detailed examination. It is an influence that invites introspection, reserve, and recollection.

The card "El Consultante" places this planet in the head, at the location of the fontanelle, the area that in newborns is still open, as their cranial bones have not yet closed. Tradition considers that reaching this energy center enables liberation from the earthly realm and the exit from the cycle of reincarnations.

This has guided me to consider this area of the person as that

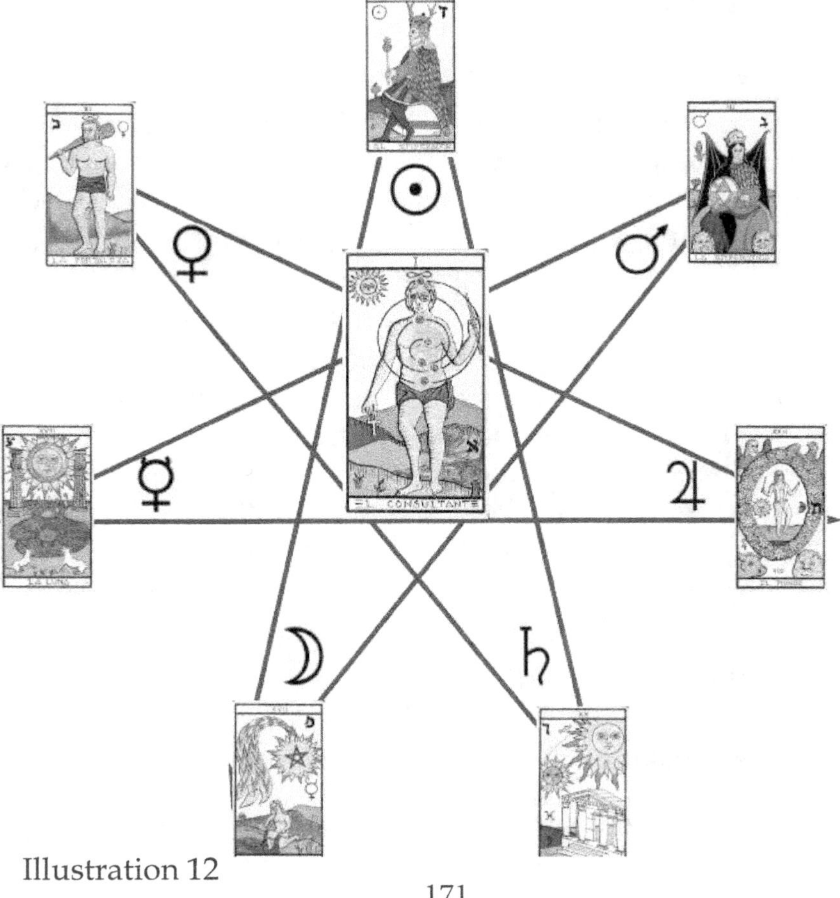

Illustration 12

related to their spiritual aspects. The dimension related to the transcendent themes in the life of a human being.

Using the cards presented in Illustration 12 as an example, I'll illustrate this spread. I have placed the card "The Consultant" in the central position, reminding us of its guiding role in this card arrangement and to keep in mind the map inscribed on its body. Surrounding this card are the following:

- "The Emperor" in the position of the Sun.
- "Strength" in the place of Venus.
- "The Moon" in the location of Mercury.
- "The Star" in the position of the Moon.
- "The Cycle" in the spot of Saturn.
- "The World" in the position of Jupiter.
- "The Empress" completes the set, placed in Mars.

After analyzing all the relationships I can see in an initial examination of the cards, the first step is to present a general overview of the consultant's situation, even if they have asked a specific question. Laying out the cards face up provides the advantage of being able to almost immediately survey the entire set.

I know other readers prefer to reveal the cards one by one, which also has its convenience, especially from the ritualistic perspective, as the act of uncovering a card often has a lot of drama. In this case, the mystery of the reading is revealed bit by bit, impacting the consultant. As the disposition of the consultant is always a factor to consider, this dose of emotion can be the element that tips the balance. It's a matter of personal preference or sometimes of assessing what may be most appropriate, depending on the consultant's disposition.

Based on the eight selected cards in the example, a possible reading would be:

The person asking the question is at the beginning of a process and has all the elements required to carry out the task, as symbolized by "The Consultant" card in the central position in the middle of the star.

"The Emperor" in the position of the Sun reinforces this idea, as this card represents mastery over material aspects. This means the consultant won't be limited by pragmatic issues, reinforced by the position of the Sun in the spread, which is the second most important position after the central one.

Continuing counterclockwise, we encounter Venus ruling the affective and partnership aspects. In this position is "Strength," suggesting a dual situation. On one hand, it indicates the energy and drive that the card's most obvious aspect suggests, and on the other hand, it invites a delicate, subtle, and gentle approach to love matters.

In Mercury's position, we find "The Moon," which suggests an introspective attitude in the main activities of the consultant. It may also warn that being overly contemplative could be detrimental in areas like business or studies.

In the area of the Moon, which relates to the realm of home and family, "The Star" is found. This card is generally a bearer of good news, and in the family context, it could indicate the arrival of a new family member. If the consultant is in a relationship and of childbearing age, it could even reveal a forthcoming child.

In the lower part and in the position of Saturn, "The Cycle" card appears. As this location is associated with transcendental and spiritual aspects, it can be interpreted that the consultant is at a moment of transition conducive to growth in this area.

In Jupiter, the planet that regulates the other gods in the Olympian pantheon and therefore embodies power, "The World" is present. This Major Arcana is the culmination of the journey that begins with "The Consultant." It symbolizes achievement, suggesting that in the sphere of power, the consultant is at a moment of fulfillment, capable of accomplishing all they undertake. Their network and relationships will provide additional support for their interests.

Completing the circle of seven cards surrounding "The Consultant," in Mars' position is "The Empress." This card depicts a mature, knowledgeable woman, suggesting that there is a person with these characteristics in the consultant's environment who will positively contribute to their pursuits.

This simplified reading is a preliminary examination that aims to provide a general perspective on the consultation's motive. What follows is a deeper inquiry exploring the relationships between the cards laid out on the spread.

Complements to the Reading of the GET

The Triangle and the Square

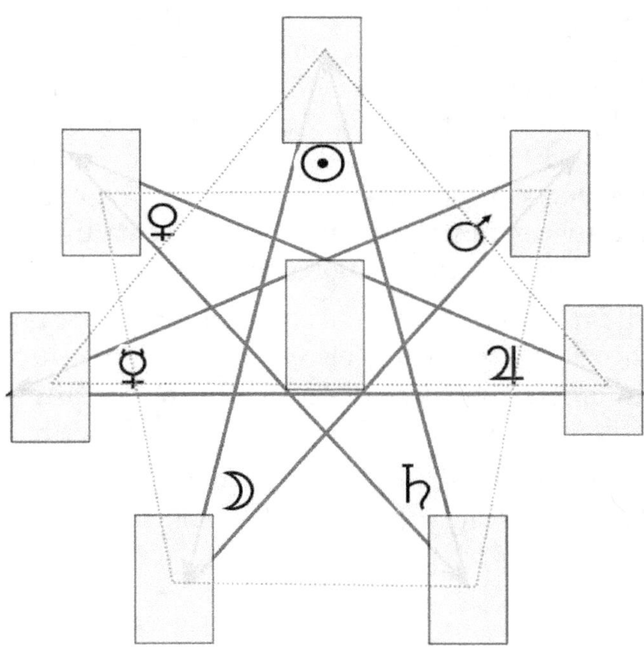

Illustration 13

Occasionally, with the aim of complementing and directing the reading towards the consultant's interests, I use the seven-pointed star spread, applying a diagram that supplements the previous distribution.

This new diagram involves classifying the seven cards located on the rays of the star into two groups:

The first group consists of cards positioned in Venus, Mars, the Moon, and Saturn. These four cards form a quadrangular figure if connected with a line, as shown by the segmented line in Illustration 13. The figure in the image is a trapezoid, to be more precise. Nevertheless, this figure can be assimilated to the symbolism of the square. As we know, the symbolism of the square is associated with the earth, the material, so I use the four cards located in this square to interpret the material aspects of the consultant's situation.

The second group includes the cards positioned in the Sun, Mercury, and Jupiter. In this case, the resulting figure when connecting these three cards with a line is a triangle. Remembering the symbolism of the triangle, we see that it represents stability, balance, and thus is associated with the more permanent or trend-like aspects of the consultant's life and, by extension, those of a more transcendental and even spiritual nature, especially if the cards in these positions suggest it.

I generally use this scheme as a complement to my usual spread, but sometimes, if circumstances require it — either due to the consultant's interest or the time available for the reading — I may use only this diagram, omitting the full content of the star spread.

In any case, the central card always plays the role of guide and represents the general situation of the consultant.

Past, Present, and Future

Another diagram that complements the use of the spread and facilitates reading involves applying the classic scheme of past, present, and future within the same spread.

To do this, I group the cards into three sets representing these three categories.

Past: Corresponds to the three cards on the left, those located in the positions of Venus, Mercury, and the Moon.

Present: I place in this category the two central cards, the one in the position of the Sun and the one in the central position, selected by the consultant.

Future: The third group corresponds to the cards on the right, those in the positions of Mars, Jupiter, and Saturn.

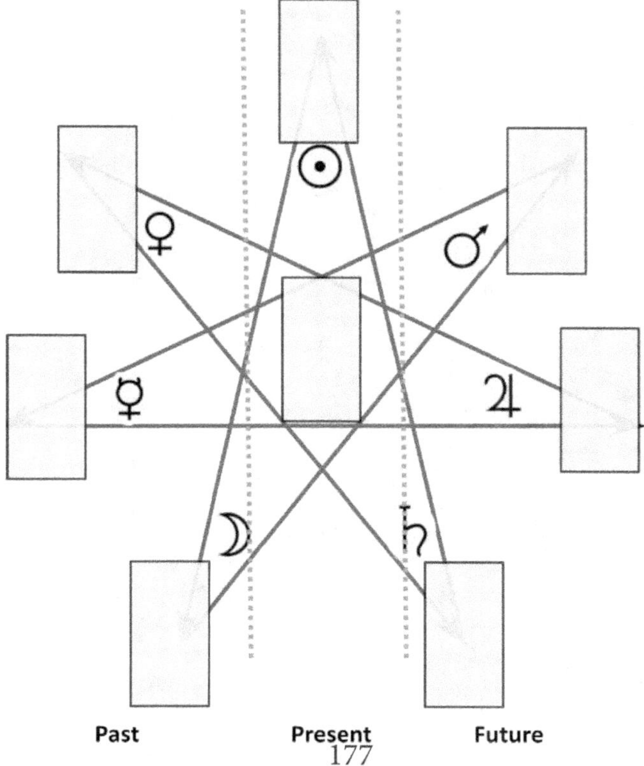

In this scheme, as always, the central card, being selected by the consultant, continues to play a predominant role in the reading and guides the entire interpretation.

When applying this approach, one can use the conceptual and symbolic framework traditionally used in triads, which at least dates back to Aristotle. The left set can be considered as the sensitive aspects, the right set as the rational characteristics, and the middle set as the synthesis of both. Similarly, the left set could be seen as the aspects against the query, the right set as the factors in favor, and the two middle cards as the result or the answer itself to the question posed.

Final Words

Tarot decks have a complex structure in their background. Particularly, decks following the tradition of the Marseille Tarot, are supported by symbolic traditions dating back to the 13th century in southern Europe.

The tarot I have presented in these pages follows the tradition of the Marseille decks, though this might not be evident at first glance. However, it almost rigorously respects this tradition, and in the few instances it deviates from the canon, it does so to add useful and innovative elements, beneficial for both beginners and advanced tarotists.

One area where the GET (Gran Tarot Esotérico) stands out from other Marseille decks is its explicit portrayal of the symbolism structuring these decks. The integration of the Hebrew alphabet and astrology in each of the major arcana provides reading clues and guides, connecting the deck to its sources.

In the case of the Hebrew alphabet, it directly connects with the Kabbalah and its primary graphical representation: the Tree of Life. As reviewed, this image of ten Sefirot is a diagram of creation and fall from a biblical standpoint, but also a path to spiritual transcendence.

The ten Sefirot of the Tree of Life are connected by 22 paths, each associated with a Hebrew letter. Eliphas Levi was the first scholar to make the connection between the arcana and the Hebrew letters, and Maritxu Guler was the first to explicitly incorporate this system into a tarot deck.

The other symbolic system incorporated is astrology. Initially, coming from a rigorous scientific background, I was somewhat reluctant to give credit to using the deck with an astrological key. However, especially after developing the spread explained in the 'Gran Tarot Esotérico' section, I began to incorporate this aspect into my readings.

For those who maintain a distance from this form of knowledge, they can dispense with the esoteric aspects of this and apply only those related to the characterology provided by astrology. Another useful aspect is the formidable excuse that astrology provides to delve into the daily life of the consultant or their circle of relationships, as we all have some approach to this topic in one way or another.

Regardless, the use of astrology is almost obligatory in this deck if using the spread I have proposed. I believe not considering it in the reader's available toolkit would be to miss out on a powerful tool the deck offers.

Therefore, I consider the GET a great option for all tarotists who want a deck that is simple, accessible, and profound at the same time.

I can only wish you to enjoy this Tarot as much as I have, as I have no doubt that in its use and exploration you will find countless rewarding surprises.

Bibliography

Altadill, J. (1883). *Un castillo navarro, derruido por el akelarre.*

Arndt, U. (2004). Revista Paracelso. *El Sendero de La Energía de La Vida: La Estrella Secreta de Siete Puntas.*

Benages, F. (2016). *Coaching y tarot. Para alcanzar la excelencia en la vida.*

Biblia de Jerusalén. (1972). *Biblia de Jerusalén.*

Bozzelli, C. (2014). *El código del tarot. Revelación de una inteligencia milenaria.* Accademia dei Tarocchi.

Eisler, R. (1990). *El cáliz y la espada* (Editorial Cuatro vientos (ed.)).

Gichtel, J. G. (2003). *Theosophia práctica.* Ediciones Obelisco.

Gimbutas, M. (1996). *El lenguaje de la diosa.* Dove.

González, F. (n.d.). *El tarot de los cabalistas.*

Graves, R. (1993). *Los Mitos Griegos Volumen II.* Alianza Editorial Madrid.

Guler, M. (1976). *El gran tarot esotérico. Libro de instrucciones.* Heraclito Fournier.

Kaplan, A. (1997). *Sefer Yetzirah.* Madrid: Editorial Mirach.

Maturana, H., & Francisco, V. (2003). *De máquinas y seres vivos. Autopoiesis: la organización de lo vivo.* Lumen.

Meegan, J. (2016). *God's Ambiance: Is revealed in the Matrix of Wisdom.* Outskirt Press.

Méndez Filesi, M. (2016a). *El tarot: 7. La Iglesia.* https://www. mmfilesi.com/tcabaret/el-tarot-7-la-iglesia/

Méndez Filesi, M. (2016b). *El tarot 6: La muerte.* https://www.

mmfilesi.com/tcabaret/el-tarot-6-la-muerte/

Méndez Filesi, M. (2016c). *El Tiempo*. https://www.mmfilesi. com/tcabaret/el-tarot-14-el-tiempo/

Murray, M. (2006). *El dios de los brujos*. Fondo de Cultura Económica.

Payne-Towler, C. (n.d.). *An Approach to Tarot History*. Retrieved November 6, 2018, from https://www.tarot.com/tarot/christine-payne-towler/history-of-tarot

Payne-Towler, C. (2006). *The Major Arcana* (p. 39).

Payne-Towler, C. (2016). *Foundations of the Esoteric Tradition: Tarot of the Holy Light*. https://www.amazon.es/Foundations-Esoteric-Tradition-Tarot-Light/dp/0967304342/ ref=sr_1_cc_3?s=aps&ie=UTF8&qid=1541464589&sr=1-3-catcorr&keywords=Christine+Payne-Towler

Perajordi, J. (1980). *La tradición astrológica*. Editorial Alas.

Rodes, D., & Sanchez, E. (2014). *El Libro de Oro. Guía práctica para la interpretación del Tarot de Marsella*. El Aleph.

Wirth, O. (1990). *The Tarot of the Magicians*. Samuel Weiser Inc.

Zimmer Bradley, M. (2000). *Las nieblas de Avalón*. Ediciones Salamandra.